Scribbles on the Wall:
Lessons Along the Way

Scribbles On The Wall

Lessons Along The Way

Evan Sutter

TENTH STREET PRESS

THIS EDITION

© **Copyright 2013 Evan Sutter**

First published by Tenth Street Press   April 2013
Second Edition   August 2013

Original cover image courtesy of Evan Sutter

ISBN: 0-9923034-2-7
ISBN13: 978-0-9923034-2-6

National Library of Australia Cataloguing-in-Publication entry

Author: Sutter, Evan, author.
Title: Scribbles on the wall : lessons along the way / Evan Sutter.

ISBN: 9780987439963 (paperback)
Subjects: Conduct of life—Anecdotes.
Self-actualization (Psychology)
Motivation (Psychology)
Compulsive behavior—Anecdotes.
Tantric Buddhism.

Dewey Number: 158.1

PRINTED IN THE U.S.A.

TENTH STREET PRESS Ltd.

MELBOURNE LONDON

www.tenthstreetpress.com
Email: contact@tenthstreetpress.com

For my Brothers

Jarrod, Nathan & Aaron Sutter

For not only your wise words which grace these pages; words which make this book much better than it otherwise would have been

But for the pieces of you that are in each word I speak

It is a lucky kid who has a mentor, coach, ally, motivator, critic, protector and best friend.

It's an even luckier one who has three.

CONTENTS

Introduction

"You do not need to know precisely what is happening, or exactly where it is all going. What you need is to recognize the possibilities and challenges offered by the present moment, and to embrace them with courage, faith and hope." Thomas Merton

In today's world people are so busy chasing after unrealistic imaginary dreams, they sacrifice today for a better tomorrow, along the way sacrificing all that is important to them, their friends and family, their passions and interests and they don't even know why; instead succumbing to the abundance of illusionary social expectations programmed into us since birth.

Our society is becoming more and more superficial and materialistic with every new ad campaign that storms into our faces, magazine covers are littered with thin, perfect-bronzed models; every ad targets our insecurities and persuades us to believe that without the latest trend we cannot be 'cool' or 'popular'. Instead of creating people of unique substance and style we encourage conformity.

The world is a messed up place. Innocent people are dying every single day, by the hands of the greedy and wicked and by the hands of disease and illness. People are unwell and suffering with chronic addiction to short term satisfaction and fast fixes, People are driven like never before by the lure of the easy money, big houses and fast cars, natural disasters sweep the planet, Hurricanes to Tsunamis to Earthquakes, people still continue to fight over age old differences, politicians still strive for votes but not change, the waves are becoming crowded and the houses expensive, the air is dirty and animals extinct.

9

People are working longer hours and spending less time with their children, new born babies are thrown straight into childcare so their parents can rush back to work, kids are diagnosed with ADHD, depression, bi polar and given quick band aid fixes, people are switching face to face communication for online and cricket bats for Xbox's.

These are the harsh realities of today and you can't control the tomorrows, all you can control is yourself and now.

These are just the many traps that can wear you down and destroy your passion and joy. For life is short, sometimes very short and we sometimes need a look at these harsh realities to drum into us the importance that all this is just temporary and we need to be grateful for the opportunities that present themselves today.

An old wise man named Socrates once said that the unconsidered life is not worth living. He meant that walking along the same path of everyone around you with no real direction, desire and passion can leave you too dependent at the hands of others and living a life without thought and reason can mean living a life with no real value.

Wise men learn from others mistakes; here is an unfinished list of mine.

Putting pleasure before happiness, friends before myself and party before discipline. Using people, alcohol and drugs. Not being brave. Thinking I cannot be happy 'now' without a girl, sex, a great job, car, house. Spending time with fools. Hurting others. Not caring enough. Not recognising real wealth. My entire life I had been searching for the wrong thing.

If we are able to quiet the cravings within us, we see that our true desire is not wealth, sex or fame, but simply peace and happiness.

The pages that follow are by no means definitive truths of the world but merely thoughts for reflection and discussion. By no means do they provide answers or are they intended to be a preaching of any kind; they are simply opinions and ideals from the wisdoms of experience and observation open for interpretation whichever way you feel fit.

I don't want people to believe I actually know what I am talking about, because actually my view is just a view among many different views.

"Success is born in every moment. To laugh often and much, to win the respect of intelligent people and the affection of children, to earn appreciation of honest critics and endure betrayal of false friends, to appreciate beauty, to find the best in others, to leave the world a bit better, whether by a healthy child, a garden patch or a redeemed social condition, to know even one life has breathed easier because you have lived well.

This is to have succeeded. Success does not come at the end of the day or year or on ones deathbed, it is born in every moment and dies in every moment". T.S Elliot

Work & Money

"Insanity is doing the same thing, over and over again, but expecting different results." Narcotics Anonymous

I was brought up by hard working blue-collar parents, I was one of four sons, at the time work was sparse and I remember my father would come home from his day job and leave straight away for a night shift at a local service station. So naturally we were brought up with strong work ethics, as soon as we turned the legal age of 14 years and 9 months we were basically told to find work, so we could enjoy the fruits of our own labour. We were told if you want something we should work hard and earn it, so we could truly appreciate it.

I think this statement is familiar for a lot of people; their parents were from a generation where this was drilled into them from birth. But this is an out dated way of thinking, new technology has opened up opportunities and alternative lifestyle and work options like never before and we shouldn't be telling our kids to get a job, just any job, we should be telling them to search for things they love and to follow their heart; this will serve them better in their pursuit of happiness.

It really confuses me and I think to myself 'why' when I see people going to the same old job they hate each day, every day for years on end, they struggle through the eight to ten hour day, the terrible traffic to and from, the poor public transport and they whinge about how much they hate it. But they never change it; they never even attempt to get themselves out of this ongoing rut, why? As Mother Teresa said "Work without love is slavery."

12

They are obviously not happy doing it, that's why they are constantly whinging, grumpy and rude. Why do they put themselves through this, surely your sanity and happiness is worth a little more. People do realise that we humans don't live forever, that today or tomorrow it can all come crashing down, and you have wasted your best years plodding along for what? To pay off the mortgage, so you can tell your friends, the ones you hardly see that you've bought a house.

The great Dalai Lama when asked what surprised him most about humanity said:

"Man, because he sacrifices his health in order to make money.

Then he sacrifices money to recuperate his health.

And then he is so anxious about the future that he does not enjoy the present;

The result being that he does not live in the present or the future;

He lives as if he is never going to die, and then dies having never really lived."

Too much focus is put on getting a job or going to university, but not enough focus is put on searching for something you love, something that you're passionate for and something you want to wake up in the morning for. The onus is put on money, prestige and status and what other people think, but it's you who will spend the forty odd years doing it.

The majority of people in the western world today have this very interesting take on things. They believe that buying a house, which really means getting a large debt

13

which you are committed to paying for the next thirty odd years is the big dream, it is drilled in them by their parents and their friends, which was drilled into them by their parents that buying this bricks and mortar is the stepping stone to great success. In all essence it is not too difficult to accomplish, just go to work, get some sort of savings history and the financial institutions will practically fall over themselves getting you to sign the dotted line.

What they don't mention is you are making a big commitment, a commitment that for some means forgoing holidays, forgoing having children, eating out at restaurants, the morning coffee even needs to go.

But the big thing it can do is destroy your flexibility and freedom and this is the biggest factor in why people drag themselves to the same old job they hate because they have these bills they need to pay, soon the stress has killed all their big dreams and passion. The flamboyance they once had and the personality and vigour they once bounced through life with is all but a distant memory.

An old parable taken from the No.1 New York Times bestseller "The 4-Hour Work Week" by Timothy Ferriss describes this perfectly.

An American businessman took a vacation to a small coastal Mexican village on doctor's orders. Unable to sleep after an urgent phone call from the office the first morning, he walked out to the pier to clear his head. A small boat with just one fisherman had docked, and inside the boat were several large yellow fin tuna. The American complimented the Mexican on the quality of the fish.

"How long did it take you to catch them?" the American asked. "Only a little while," the Mexican replied in surprisingly good English. "Why don't you stay out longer
14

and catch more fish?" the American then asked. "I have enough to support my family and give a few to friends," the Mexican said as he unloaded them into a basket. "But…What do you do with the rest of your time?"

The Mexican looked up and smiled. "I sleep late, fish a little, play with my children, take a siesta with my wife, Julia, and stroll into the village each evening, where I sip wine and play guitar with my amigos. I have a full and busy life, senor."

The American laughed and stood tall. "Sir, I'm a Harvard M.B.A and can help you. You should spend more time fishing, and with the proceeds, buy a bigger boat. In no time, you could buy several boats with the increased haul. Eventually, you would have a fleet of fishing boats."

He continued, "Instead of selling your catch to a middleman, you would sell directly to the consumers, eventually opening your own cannery. You would control the product, processing, and distribution. You would need to leave this small fishing village, of course, and move to Mexico City, then to Los Angeles, and eventually New York City, where you could run your expanding enterprise with proper management.

The Mexican fisherman asked, "But, senor; how long will all this take?" To which the American replied, "15-20 years. 25 tops." "But what then senor?" The American laughed and said, "That's the best part. When the time is right, you would announce an IPO and sell your company stock to the public and become very rich. You would make millions." "Millions, senor? Then what?"

"Then you would retire and move to a small coastal fishing village, where you would sleep late, fish a little, play with your kids, take a siesta with your wife, and stroll to a village
15

in the evenings where you could sip wine and play guitar with your amigos…"
Does it make sense to do something you don't like for thirty years?

Does it make sense to do something you don't like for thirty days?

Does it make sense to push yourself through the slog of everyday monotonous for a long period of time, sacrificing your health and your relationships so you can achieve the 'Great Western World Dream' of owning your own home, which you are free to enjoy just when you require your first hip replacement on the eve of your first overseas trip.

I find it sad when you talk to people and you ask them what they have been up to and they respond with just working because they just bought a house. They seem lacklustre and lifeless; they give up the things they love like surfing and simple things like catching up with mates for a beer because they have too many bills to pay. Maybe they have over exerted themselves financially, maybe they believe making these sacrifices now will make for a better tomorrow, but as the Dalia Lama said the tomorrows might never come and if they do you might not be in the state to enjoy it.

It wasn't too long ago that the word career was unheard of now it's all too common; it's pushed through schools and the education system by parents and teachers and by the media. Just like the mortgage it's branded and positioned as this beacon of success and status and people are willing to drive themselves through pain to get there sacrificing their dreams and loves along the way. Careers mean guaranteed taxes each year for the government and mortgages mean rates and people needing to stay in careers; a win-win situation for the government and the economy.

It's all too common hearing stories of people who have worked their backsides off setting up a house and future for their family and just before retirement when they can finally relax and enjoy it, they get sick and pass away. But even with these stories people still plod along in undesirable jobs through necessity and fear of the unknown.

It's about finding the balance in all aspects of life and especially in work. Too much of one extreme is dangerous and it seems that a lot of people are struggling to find a healthy balance. Some years ago, my first job out of university I drove to work each day through traffic sometimes taking two hours one way. I did this for almost two years, I would look at the other faces in the driver's seats around me and see stress and anger and I would think to myself 'why anyone would do this'. I saw a total lack of emotion from people older than me as if a sign that they had already given up, and then and there I said 'I will never do that to myself'.

Of course it was a far more difficult prospect than I thought and over the years I have fallen back into the trap of fighting traffic and poor public transport conditions in order to make some money. Still I see on the news the traffic build up day in day out and I think to myself how glad I am that I stayed true to myself and I can't help but laugh as to why people would put themselves through absolute torture. It's obvious it's not enjoyable; it's plain to see that it is not good for your health but it is still happening every day in every city. Do they even know why they are doing this? Why they are putting themselves through it? Or do they think they are going to live forever?

It is paramount that more onus is put on finding love and

passion in the things you do and finding a lifestyle that allows you to find the balance to enjoy the things you love, whether this means quitting your stressful job in the big smoke now and moving to the country where you have always wanted to instead of waiting till you retire, as this day may never come, maybe it means your current role isn't available there so you work in another area, just enough so you can actually enjoy your life with the ones you love. Maybe it means selling your home and down grading so you can work less hours and have more free time, maybe it means a different job, a new company, maybe it means getting rid of that pricey gym membership you never use and instead dusting off the surfboard or going for a jog outside.

You need to realise that there are always options and whilst making changes can be challenging and difficult we cannot afford to let fear dictate what we do and hold us back from moving forward. We need to look at quality of life a job provides and not just focus on the dollar signs. We need to narrow down exactly what it is in our jobs that is dulling our energy and make changes. Is it long hours, travel time, poor work culture, unsupportive co – workers, is it being underpaid or unappreciated, mundane routine and lack of creativity? Making small changes might be enough to make more drastic changes in the balance of your life. Moving to a new position could provide greater flexibility in working hours and more suited co-workers, relocating closer to home might mean a little less cash each week but might mean forgoing sitting in the car for twenty hours each week and being home earlier to spend time with the kids.

This example was never more evident than in one of my best friends. He went straight from school into university and straight into a big company smack bang in the middle

18

of the city CBD. After about 6 months it was clear that he disliked the role intensely, it was nothing what he thought, mundane routine, long hours, unsupportive co-workers, unfriendly environment. But everyone he spoke to said to stick with it, it's just the natural process when you start; they told him it's a great big company with endless potential for him. So he stuck it out, another year went by and the job not only was effecting him at work but it was dulling his exuberance and personality out of it, his once bubbly outgoing character was replaced with a guy now void of positivity.

He was in a very difficult position, he was working for a well- known company in a good position and everyone around him was so proud; from the outside he looked like he was well on the path to great success but for him personally it was a much different story. He didn't know what to do, it was his first job out of University and he wondered if this was how it was meant to be, was this just normal work life.

It took a very strong, courageous young man to finally listen to his heart and resign despite the expectations and the talk that said otherwise. Over the years he moved from one job to another, experiencing different roles in different organisations, he studied another short course totally unrelated to his previous business related degree, he started to travel to a few new places and relocated a few times. It wasn't too long before his old love for life and immense passion came back to greet us and this time it felt somewhat more real. Because this time it was backed by greater confidence, more experiences and more perspective and new found meaning.

The one change in work life had an almost immediate impact on the rest of his life. He was no longer in an
19

uninspiring relationship, he travelled overseas for the first time, he found a new lifestyle that better suits, he's got passions and interests and an overall new drive for life. He's now in a job he loves that quite ironically makes more money than he ever could have before and most importantly he's the happiest I've ever seen him. It was a tough initial decision to make, he took a big risk and he upset a lot of people by doing it, but it was a decision that only he could make because he's the only one who has to do it each day and it's the best decision he has ever made, one decision that took his entire life down a total different path.

It's about not comparing what you have and what you do with someone else because you will end up paying for it, in this case for fifty years; so take your time and find your passion. Follow your heart and its true desires and as Confucius said "Choose a job you love and you will never have to work a day in your life."

But obviously finding this 'dream' job can prove just as ambitious and vexed as finding the overall balance in all aspects of life. Whilst waiting patiently can serve you well, sometimes getting another job can get you closer to your ideal situation and keep you moving forward, allowing you to have a good time whilst you are waiting. Because let's face it we all need money to do the things we love and any job can provide the funds to allow us to go on road trips surfing up the coast, or bungee jumping, or restoring that old car. The last thing we want to do is waste all our time just waiting for that dream gig to just pop into our laps because in reality it's not that pretty.

Wasted time manifests into regret and regrets are a lazy man's thoughts, so keep moving forward with one eye on the main prize whilst doing the things you love with the

20

people you love and don't allow the hecticness of life to stray you off your path.

"I do not particularly like the word 'work.' Human beings are the only animals who have to work, and I think that is the most ridiculous thing in the world. Other animals make their livings by living, but people work like crazy, thinking that they have to in order to stay alive. The bigger the job, the greater the challenge, the more wonderful they think it is. It would be good to give up that way of thinking and live an easy, comfortable life with plenty of free time. I think that the way animals live in the tropics, stepping outside in the morning and evening to see if there is something to eat, and taking a long nap in the afternoon, must be a wonderful life. For human beings, a life of such simplicity would be possible if one worked to produce directly his daily necessities. In such a life, work is not work as people generally think of it, but simply doing what needs to be done." Masanobu Fukuoka, the One – Straw Revolution

Travel, Exploration & Adventure

"Adventure is a path. Real adventure – self-determined, self-motivated, often risky – forces you to have firsthand encounters with the world. The world the way it is, not the way you imagine it. Your body will collide with the earth and you will bear witness. In this way you will be compelled to grapple with the limitless kindness and bottomless cruelty of humankind – and perhaps realize that you yourself are capable of both. This will change you. Nothing will ever again be black-and-white." Mark Jenkins

If I could wish you do one thing, I wish for you to travel the world, to explore new places and new cultures, to get lost, to be scared, to be totally out of your comfort zone. My first big trip overseas was for me the single greatest thing I have ever done. It totally changed the man I am today, gave me great new insights of the world, but more importantly made me see myself in a whole new light.

Travel opens up a world of possibility, a world of opportunity. New people and new places, It's hard to explain the effect waking up in a new county or city can have on someone, each day is filled with a fresh start, the mistakes of the past simply disappear, you somewhat feel like a new person on a new journey.

Some people argue people travel to escape, to escape their mundane, plateau like existence; quite frankly it's not a bad reason at all. You never know what a look at the world can offer, what it can do to change someone's attitudes, goals and existence. For me travelling overseas has had the single biggest impact and influence on my life, more than anything else. More so than 13 years of schooling and 4 years of university, more than any book I've ever read or
22

exam I've ever passed, more than any words of advice I've ever been given.

It's difficult to explain the effect of landing in a new continent, on the other side of the world, with nothing but a good mate and a backpack. It's hard to explain how you still remember the smell the first time you stepped outside, how you still have the most distinct image and how you felt like you've never felt before. How with that one inhale of foreign air, somewhat of a new man was born, a man filled with nothing but positivity, nothing but optimism, opportunity and ridiculous levels of excitement.

My friends, who have travelled whether it is just a few short-term trips domestic or overseas, have a distinct difference about them when compared to those who didn't. It's recognisable in their confidence and in their outlook on life. They seem more open to things and less stuck in their ways, they are able to embrace change, rather than let stress build and build and then dictate terms. They gain greater independence, from the time of having to book flights, trains, buses, ferry's, accommodation, buy food, look after your belongings, understand new languages, read maps, read timetables and manage your money across currencies. You have to do it, no one does it for you, and it's amazing how quickly you adapt to life that way, if you don't you simply don't have a place to stay, or don't have anything to eat.

Some Tips

-      Don't have an exact plan, don't book days in advance and definitely not weeks in advance, you never know if you will love a place and want to stay longer, you never know who you will meet with offers of accommodation or cool adventures and adversely you might realise the hotel you booked looks nothing like the pictures and you want to get out of there right away.

- Contiki tours and other bus about tours are for girls only or if you are a first time traveller, travelling solo. Don't let others dictate what you do and when you do it, it takes away the joys of travel and the meaning of adventure and discovery, just like the point above, you are booked in for the month, day in day out. You don't want to be walking out of the Lowenbrau tent in Oktoberfest, one of the world's biggest festivals, with a good crew all heading back to an after weisen party (weisen is the local name for Oktoberfest) and you have to bail because your bus leaves for Berlin Tomorrow at 430am. Add to that travel is about meeting new people from other countries and other cultures, on these tours you end up spending all your time with other people from the same country in large groups and miss out on the little intricacies and beauty of other cultures. "The value of your travels does not hinge on how many stamps you have in your passport when you get home -the slow nuanced experience of a single country is always better than the hurried, superficial experience of forty countries." Rolf Potts

- Leave your pre conceived ideas and expectations at the door, there's good and bad in every country

- Pack light, you can pick up what you need pretty much everywhere.

- Get into it and have a crack, immerse yourself, eat foods you never would and dance like you never have.

-    Say hello, don't sit in the corner by yourself, you are in another country, maybe on the other side of the world, people love new things and things that are different. Trust me, they will want to speak to you and you never know what adventure it could lead to.

-    Don't ask for directions and take it as concrete, ask someone else too, otherwise you will end up walking in the opposite direction for hours no closer to your destination. Lots of things get lost in translation, always have a rough idea and ask just as a precaution. In saying that, getting lost is fun.

-    If you're running short on cash and don't have any deodorant, simply lift your arms as you walk into the wind, we did it whilst backpacking through Europe, it doesn't work, but someone will notice your stupidity and give you some.

-    In this world it's far too common seeing people so quick to throw what they're doing online, on Facebook and twitter. Just enjoy the present moment and enjoy where you are at and what you are doing, you don't need to tell your friend back home you saw this or ate that. Travel is for your own self- discovery and own adventures, if you spend your time posting statuses and pictures you will miss out on many splendid opportunities.

The Must Do's

India & Thailand

As soon as we left the airport it was as if we entered a war zone, lights flashing, horns blaring, cars going in every direction, up gutters, through parks, police blew whistles and directed traffic unsuccessfully, the smell was overwhelming, the noises overbearing, we held tightly onto our seats, our faith placed in the hands of the taxi driver, as he plunged up and down gutters somewhat trying to impress us with his speed and handling; he spoke no English and we had no idea where we were headed but the world around us had consumed us.

Like no place I've ever been, in that one 20 minute cab ride, Delhi, India had opened our eyes to a completely new world, one in which cardboard boxes replaced apartments, homes to the millions of poor, one in which anarchy replaced order and a one in which our prior conceptions were totally destroyed.

India is a cool place, it's not normally on the radar for must see spots, but if there was a spot in the world that can open your eyes and make you realise how fortunate you are, its India. The crowds are hectic, the smells overwhelming and the people out of this world. They are cricket mad, amongst other things. I had what seemed like the whole school line up to bowl to me in a game of before school cricket, everywhere you look, every patch of vacant land, grass or dirt or concrete is taken up by a game of cricket, the boys and girls full of smiles, despite the poverty that surrounds them. Endless beggars patrol the streets, young children, the elderly, lepers and the sick, looking and searching for food and money.

26

India is a country of many contrasts, the poorest of poor, next to the mega rich, the crowded cities and the uncrowded coastal towns, filled with Europeans escaping their winters; surfing, fishing and partying.

Thailand is a special place. Don't get stuck in the tourist trap of Phuket and walk away thinking this is Thailand. Because Thailand is much more than overweight Aussies and Geezers with what look like 16 year old Thai girls. Get out and explore, get off the usual tourist run, get to Railay, Ton Sai and Chiang Mai. And don't fear the street food man, the banana pancakes are to this day, the 2nd best thing I've ever had in my mouth.

I went to visit a mate who was living in Bangkok, the capital of Thailand; from there it was planned that he would take me on a little local knowledge adventure around various parts of Thailand. Turns out the night before my flight is set to depart Sydney I receive an email stating he was delayed with work in Nice, France and would be a few weeks before his return to 'Bangers'.

I'm not going to lie I was pretty scared with the thought of travelling solo in a place I had no idea and trying to fill in the time for two possibly three weeks. I called up a few mates who had been around there before to get an idea of spots to go to, as now I would be without my tour guide/safety net.

With weeks to spare and no plan whatsoever I thought this would be a good test of confidence and character none the less. It made me realise that travelling solo is an amazing education and a lesson that should be compulsory for everyone. If you want to test someone's substance and independence then this is the perfect examination. We should all send our kids and young family on one of these compulsory adventures; here's where we will see how strong, confident and wise they are. It will test more aspects of their personality and character than any University degree and is much more than half the price.

I took everything with the flow, flights, buses, motorbikes, long hikes, accommodation and saw plenty of the different sides of Thailand, and there are plenty. When solo you open yourself up to more adventures, you kick around with people you otherwise may not and end up in places you wouldn't even think.

You find the main difference when travelling in groups or with a few mates you tend to stick to your group at dinner or the bar to a certain extent, when solo, there's no hiding behind any mates because you stand out in the crowd and find yourself on the receiving end of plenty of invites as a result.

I was initially scared, more so about figuring out what I was going to do to pass the time, but this fear soon dissipated very quickly and the freedom and endless options where absolutely liberating. The places I saw I honestly don't know I would have found if I was with friends, maybe this is because you are more compelled to explore to fill the time rather than share in a familiar and safe conversation.

But Thailand is a great place with so much more to it than just the main tourist hubs, the people are beautiful and the food amazing.

When I finally caught up with my mate back in Bangkok I felt like I was away on a two year trip, confident, outgoing and secure; a different man to the boy who was scared, shy and nervous just two weeks earlier. The adventure I then had with my mate around the city of Bangkok was just as special, he showed me the 'real' Bangkok and that is an incredible place with adventures galore to be had.

Portugal - Why it pays to have no plans

We made our way up the coast, about one hour north of Lisbon, the Capital of Portugal, we weren't too sure what we would find, but we needed a break from the big cities, we jumped on a bus, myself and my Australian travelling partner, and two Canadians who like us had a broad plan and plenty of time. We found ourselves in the middle of the European Surfing Championship, somehow made friends with a South African Professional Surfer, who was living in Portugal, who subsequently was beaten first round.

Somehow a plan was hatched to jump in his camper van, alongside his 13 surfboards and road trip down the coast. For the next 3 weeks an amazing adventure erupted, Two Australians, two Canadians and one South African, complete strangers one day, and great mates the next. We surfed, fished, camped in secluded coves, made friends with hash smoking German gypsies, and survived a near drowning in freezing waters whilst exploring a pretty special foreign land.

We were welcomed to stay at his house on return, owned by his surf sponsors, there we ate every day for free amongst local Portuguese and Brazilians in their café, played poker in high rise apartments over the beach with locals, went to secret local's only beach parties with far too many beautiful people and far too many Caparinha's. It's funny by allowing some freedom in your life; you truly do open yourself up to amazing opportunities and adventures.

The U.S.A

It took me some time to get over to the states. Once I got there, I questioned, why it took so long. The states are a very cool spot, each state offering something a little different to the next.

Vegas

Every man should do at least 2 nights in Las Vegas, there probably isn't any reason to do anymore, after the 1st night, you will know why. Vegas gives new meaning to 24/7, the casinos are mirror images at 7am as they are at 7pm, it's around the clock entertainment, party and fun. Again, here the notion of no plans will bear fruit, you will meet so many people, get invites to so many parties, don't brush them off because you had plans, go with the flow and you will end up in some pretty memorable situations. At night there are endless options and by day, god gave us pool parties. Anything goes, but maintain your smarts.

Las Vegas is a single man's Mecca, and every single man should head there for a quick few days of guilt stricken pleasure. It's little wonder it's the hotspot for bucks parties for people all over the world and should you be worried when your fiancé tells you he's thinking about heading to Vegas for his last hurrah… maybe….

There's a plethora of nightclubs and bars scattered all around the desert cities casinos, they are flash, super modern and out of this world and they are all action any night of the week.

Pool parties are a big deal during the days in Vegas and unless you're into shopping they are the only real option after that big night before. The intense illness you feel from the activities the night before will quickly dissipate as you bask in the wonders of beautiful people from all over the world with everyone primed for nothing but good times at any cost. Before you know it the day will have merged with night and you're back on your way to another beautiful, wild, crazy adventure in the appropriately named sin city.

New Orleans

New Orleans is one part of the states that is unique in itself; you won't see it anywhere else, Great music and great food. It can get pretty wild and off the two main streets you can find yourself in some trouble after dark. Muggings and shootings are everyday occurrences. Don't drink too much and wander off into the dark like at home, we did, and needless to say, we are extremely lucky that we weren't the gators brekky, never to be heard or seen from again. Cool joint, but keep your wits about you.

The detailed story of how my mate and I survived a robbery attempt can be seen in the drugs and alcohol section. Our naivety teamed up nicely with our great inebriated state which placed us in a very precarious situation, the recount is very much movie like, running through a neighborhood where we have no idea, jumping fences as bullets fly past our heads, luckily for us we found a savior in a man opening up a McDonalds restaurant, he opened the doors and locked us in, where we ate hash browns and waited for the police to arrive, which they never did, as they were probably too busy being called out to people who weren't so lucky.

But that's travel; it opens you up to some inconceivable
31

and crazy adventures, adventures that you can never imagine or plan, things that just happen when you're on the road with clear heads and open minds.

The California coast from L.A to Mexico

This is synonymous with summertime and beach culture around the world, the surf, the sun, music and girls. Head to Pacific Beach San Diego, nothing else needs to be said.

One of the great things about travel is the community that it creates. Once you have travelled and seen and experienced firsthand the amazing generosity of complete strangers it starts the cycle that you in turn are more than willing to reciprocate.

I told my friend who lives in North Carolina of my plans to head to San Diego on my way back to L.A and then home to Sydney. He told me he had a mate who lived there, with nothing more said he had planned for his mate to pick me up from the airport. There I stood out the front of San Diego airport only knowing his name and that he drove a big white truck. After an hour or so, a big white 'ute' pulled up, the driver yelled out "are you Evan?" and just like that a another pretty cool adventure took place. One in which started with a straight pull into the pub and after six or so beers and about the same amount of shots I had made myself a new mate and met about another 10 or so locals, I had learnt about the place, had a place to stay and plenty of options for the night and days ahead.

It's funny because when you're at home stuck in routine and the work life you wouldn't think of hanging out with a stranger down the road, but when travelling your spirit becomes free and open to all possibilities. I really fell in

32

love with Pacific Beach in San Diego, so much so that I even considered missing my flight home for my cousins wedding. There's certain places you come across where you know you have unfinished business and you know you will be back again and this is just one of mine.

Samoa

If you get the chance on your travels to catch up with a local, whether it be an old friend, a friend of a friend, an old enemy even, take it, trust me, local knowledge makes your travels that much sweeter. I was lucky enough to hook up with a few mates family in Samoa in the South Pacific and have one of the best months of my life. I was welcomed to the village with pigs, which in turn I had to track down and kill then cook it on the customary fire known as an 'umu'. Local fishing spots, surf spots, local waterfalls and swimming holes, BBQ's and massive cook ups made possible from a little bit of local knowledge. Samoa is great, forget the renowned tourist places like Fiji and Bali where you spend most of your time with other tourists anyway; get outside the square and check out some untouched paradises.

Munich, Germany

You must go to Munich during Oktoberfest, The world's largest fair, over 6 million people, 16 or so days, 100,000 seats in 14 halls, in the 42 hectare showground. It simply can't be missed, it is super good times. Regardless of whether you drink or not, it is a massive event that takes over the city, filling it with an amazing vibe, it is flooded with people from all over the world, and the streets are
33

abuzz with live music, dancing and great food.

It is hard to explain the feeling when you barge your way into one of the halls on the opening day, search for your seat and wait impatiently for the tapping of the first keg to kick start the celebrations. And that's what it is, it's a huge celebration, everyone in extremely high spirits, think Christmas, new year's, Australia day and a few music festivals rolled into one, and that's a little taste of what Munich brings in late September. Over 6,900,000 litres of beer is consumed over the days and some 58,000 Pork knuckles, but forget that, the atmosphere is electrifying, both inside and outside the halls and it is very easy to let yourself get lost in the spirit of things.

The Germans sing in their native tongue, "We are drinking, we are drinking, we are drinking to our health", and while that seems quite ironic with the damage they are doing to their bodies, I think that in essence they are, anytime that you can get together with thousands upon thousands of your fellow man, and sing, and laugh, and eat good food and drink very good beer then surely your health is benefiting.

The Germans whilst commonly renowned for their amazing innovation in regards to the motor vehicle, their greatest innovation is undoubtedly the strap that joins their body to the table so when they finally pass out after 14 days and litres upon litres of stein, they don't fall to the ground causing any undue damage to themselves, they simply rest in a very comfortable, hammock like position.

If I must give some advice, that is don't spend one night at the festival, and just spend it in the beer hall, yes, it will be an amazing, unforgettable lifelong experience, but the festival is much, much more. Spend at least a few days in Munich, one day off the drink and cruise around outside

34

the halls, tasting the food and there is an abundance of amazing food, maybe jump on a few rides, maybe kick back and really look at the people around you, the dress, the accents, take in the carnival atmosphere.

After that spend a night in Munich, Munich is a super cool city anytime of the year, especially around the Oktoberfest, it is flooded with people from all over the world, and the streets are abuzz with live music and dancing, the pubs are full and have the same vibe as any beer hall inside the showground. Only then, and only then will you truly get the feel of Oktoberfest and Munich, and Germany and the German people, and after all, that is what travelling is all about, taking in the real culture and seeing the real people.

Morocco, Nth Africa

I had always heard great things about Morocco, so many things about its amazing diversity, culture and great surfing spots. As we drove down the west coast of Europe through France, Spain and Portugal we couldn't wait to get across the strait of Gibraltar that separates Spain in Europe and Morocco in Africa. Of course we had to be patient as our 1983 Ford Bedford had a top speed of 80km/hr. After being held in customs in Morocco for hours as they searched are car for guns we eventually were spared further torture after we struck up a good conversation with one of the policeman and offered him my book 'Into the Wild' to help him continue his education of English. His English mustn't have been too productive as I never received the email he said he would send when he completed it.

But what I learnt from Morocco is that when travelling you can see two total different sides to a place and have
35

some very contrasting experiences. From a driving perspective we saw all the places between the places people go to see, we saw all the people in between the places people go to see and some of it wasn't pretty.

Our English van stood out like a sore thumb (quite a silly saying, a sore thumb doesn't really stand out, but I'll run with it) and every time we stopped we were confronted on every window by groups of people, groups of people who were absolutely no where 2 minutes earlier as we drove through nothing, but would suddenly appear whenever we thought we'd found a good spot.

To cut a long story short, the top speed of 80km mixed with intense heat and constant badgering meant we didn't even make it south enough to reach the surf spots before we decided to head back to safety. Quite luckily as what happened next, literally minutes after reaching Europe was the most intense, unbelievable food poisoning we've all ever had. And you couldn't pick a better spot for it to happen, with four men in a small van and no toilet, which sat upon a hill in northern France as we decided that room, would be much better suited as storage for the surfboards.

This is another great thing about travel; no matter how bad at the time, it is these memories that make you laugh and smile every time you catch up with your mates and it is these times that shape you as a person; when you are completely out of your comfort zone and quite literally shitting yourself.

Evan Sutter

The East Coast of Australia

In Australia's backyard, you have in your hands arguably the greatest stretch of coastline on the entire planet. The summer time road trip is a necessity. Surfing, fishing, the camp fire, live music, packed bars and pubs, beautiful women, the blazing sun and sea breeze, good mates and good food make for some incredible adventures. Seal Rocks, Crescent Head, Yamba, Byron Bay, the Gold Coast, Maroochydore, 1770, Airlie Beach, Cairns. The list goes on and on. Pack the cars, get the boys in tow and get ready for some good times. If you're lucky enough to get yourself on a west coast road trip, be sure to discover the beauty of Margaret River, for its surf, coast line and surrounding Vineyards.

If you're on the East Coast road trip, be sure to stop in one of these.

-    Beach Hotel, Byron Bay

 I've travelled to many places around the world and in summertime, I don't know if there is a place anywhere that has bragging rights over Byron. The town itself has an abundance of amazing food, amazing people and a super cool vibe.

Across the road from main beach, people flock to the beach hotel. Don't be surprised to see semi clothed beauties from all over the globe lying down on the grass whilst having a beverage, and as the sun goes down, and some funky sounds hit the stage, the mood is one of energy, fun and chilled out good times.

I've had some pretty cool times at the beachy, on any day

of the week, whether for a quiet beer or not so quiet, it's a mix of cool, like-minded people from all over the world in one place, everyone embracing the holiday feel. If you haven't spent one night or ten at the beach hotel in Byron bay, then what are you doing.

-       Pacific Hotel, Yamba

If you're doing a road trip up or down the east coast, then jumping off the highway 30mins to Yamba is a must. And one of the must do's is stopping into the Pacific Hotel.

Perched high above the town, with amazing views of the Pacific Ocean, sit back and chill out in laid back atmosphere of the pacific hotel. Having a beer, a nice meal, listening to some live music, with some pretty special views and the smell of the ocean, is the perfect end to a day of sun and surf.

-       North Gong Hotel, North Wollongong

On a cracking summer's day, the North 'Gong' is the place to be when down south. Sitting outside, taking in the rays, one thing is certain and that is some very good times.

 The amount of beautiful people who get down there is easily noticed, and the mood is fun and can get very wild. Kicking off at the North Gong is probably a safe bet that it will turn into something much bigger, it is the perfect prelude before the city run later. If you happen to snag a North gong mission on Australia day, and it happens to be a Sunday, then you're are in for one of the best nights on any coast in Australia.

Evan Sutter

- The Brewery, Newcastle

Out the back of the Brewery in summer time is not to be missed. When a cool band is playing, and the sun soaring, sitting just metres from the water's edge, it is Sunday Session Heaven.

It has a cool vibe with a cool crew of people, whether for a few lazy beers before work on Monday or as the entrée before the big night out, it is the perfect end to any week and one of the must do's when in Newcastle and the Hunter region.

- Shoal Bay Country Club, Shoal Bay

Just a short one hour drive north from Newcastle you will come to Nelson Bay and its surrounding suburbs, one in which is Shoal Bay, which just happens to be one of the most beautiful spots on the entire east coast.

It is paradise for the outdoors person with plenty of bushwalking and mountain bike trails, good secluded surf spots, pristine sands and crystal clear waters, grassy mountains and plenty of sea life.

And you will be privy to all of this from the Shoal Bay Country club, out the front you have some the best views around; not a bad spot to have a cold beer and relax.

- Hotel Brunswick, Brunswick Heads

Just North of Byron Bay and the famous Beach Hotel is a small town called Brunswick Heads. It's a town with a hippy and country feel and the local Hotel encompasses all
39

of it. The pub gets some cool bands and is a great stop over for lunch or dinner.

- Lennox Head Pub, Lennox Head

Just 15 minutes south of Byron Bay lays its little brother, Lennox Head and the Lennox head hotel is a great spot to stop in on your way up or down the coast.

The Lennox gets some good bands with a small town feel and out the front are some of the best waves in the world.

- Beaches Merewether, Newcastle

Arguably there is no better spot for an afternoon beer or lunch whilst in the Hunter. Merewether is the king of Newcastle's surf beaches and you see it all perched high on the hill at the Beaches Hotel.

Great spot outside in summer and despite some new competition from hotels in the area, the beaches still has that cool, relaxed atmosphere like no other.

- Coogee Bay Hotel, Coogee

Coogee is one of the homes to the abundance of British and European backpackers that hit Australia's shores each year and they can be found at the Coogee bay hotel on any night of the week.

Coogee is the coast meets city, it's not the quiet night out relaxing by the water and the place gets pretty heavy and crazy, but if you're in for a fun night with plenty of people from all walks of life from around all corners of the globe
40

get down to the Coogee Bay Hotel.

- Newport Arms, Newport

Newport Arms is sophistication meets beauty. When on the north side of Sydney, the Newport Arms is a must; not only because it's great spot, but for the people, the environment and the food.

- Wharf Bar, Manly

The Wharf Bar is the big player on the other side of the bridge of Sydney. It not only is a great spot location wise it is a great spot for people too. The 'Wharfy' as it is affectionately known is a hub for good looking people and good times in general. It is renowned for its Sunday sessions and with good reason.

Disregarding all the mentioned benefits that travelling can provide, it is fun, good fun. You can have the time of your life and have memories that stick with you for an eternity. It will make you laugh, and make you smile, and anything that can do that should be strongly encouraged.

A look at the history of the Berlin wall, the sound of an old windmill in Bruges, the sweetness of a paella in Barcelona, the wildness of a soccer match in Lisbon, the quaint view from top a Greek island, the crazy cultures of Amsterdam, the power of the colosseum in Rome, the smiles Surfing till 10pm on the coast of France before getting into a 30cent bottle of red, enduring the chaos of Marrakech, being taken over by the snow-capped
41

mountains of Austria, living the party at Oktoberfest, feeling the melancholy of the west front, understanding the accents in Dublin, enjoying a welsh cake in Wales, hearing the sweet sounds of a church choir in Samoa, fearing for a beggar in Mumbai, appreciating the beauty of Margaret River, basking in a beer in Byron Bay.

From no plan at all, to meeting people from all parts of the globe, heading to places you never thought you would, it is truly an amazing journey, adventure, exploration. One that can't be imagined conceived or believed. Exploring and discovering new lands and new people whilst simultaneously discovering yourself.

Travel is amazing for a range of things and for relationships especially. Echoing the words from Mark Twain there is no surer way to find out whether you like people or hate them than to travel with them.

If you want to find out about someone you quickly find that out on the road, mates who you have known for years and years are seen in new light and the girlfriend or boyfriend are quickly seen at their worst and their best.

On a recent trip to the U.S.A with four good mates I have known for over fifteen years this was never more evident.

There was the one who became known as 'Sloth Monster' for his perfecting of over sleeping and over eating, one such night we woke suddenly thinking he was being sick after a big night as he reached for the brown paper bag, only to realize seconds later that he was merely immersing himself into a leftover slice of pepperoni pizza which couldn't wait till morning.

There was 'Mirrors', who would take hours in the bathroom before heading out, who had five different kinds of hair product and if that wasn't enough he would take subtle and not so subtle glances at anything that could give off even the slightest of reflections – shop front windows, passing cars, a couple seconds each time we jumped in a taxi; so much so it wouldn't surprise me if he caught himself in spoons at the café and other peoples sunglasses.

There was 'Snappy'; who would out of the blue 'snap' into a rage of fury and a plethora of expletives, then transform into normality as quickly as it began, later apologizing for his actions.

And there was 'Garbo' who would happily finish off everyone's plate regardless of the state it was in. After a few days all plates would automatically be passed over to his side when we were done eating and without a word Garbo would accommodate.

I travelled with a friend in Europe for six months; I quickly found out that he was the world's worst dancer and quite quirky, but also one of the kindest, nicest, most genuine guys I had ever had the pleasure of meeting.

I had known all the boys closely for so long but had limited experience with them day in day out for over a month straight. You see personality traits that you wouldn't in everyday life; you see them in between all the good times. You can't hide something from others when you're living in their pocket every hour of everyday, eventually your true colours come out for all to see and that is exactly why it should be heavily encouraged to go travelling with your girlfriend or boyfriend before you commit to something long term.

Because travel is a better indicator and gives a truer picture then living with someone ever will.

You get the privilege of seeing your closest friends open and bare, you get to dig deep and see exactly why they are such great people in all their little intricate idiosyncrasies and you get to realize how lucky you are and the important part they play in your life.

Travel is an education in all aspects of life and especially in the education of you as an individual.

Cesare Pavese hit the nail on the head when he said "Traveling is a brutality. It forces you to trust strangers and to lose sight of all that familiar comfort of home and friends. You are constantly off balance. Nothing is yours except the essential things: air, sleep, dreams, sea and the sky."

So, save up some money, sacrifice the short term for the long term, plan with some mates, or bite the bullet and face it solo, set a date, have a rough idea of where you want to go, and do it. It doesn't need to be any more complicated. Jump on that plane, that bus, ferry, train, car or hitchhike and enjoy what the world has to offer you.

Sex, Girls & Marriage

"Last time I had sex I was so good I got a standing ovation. Well, actually, I just got the clap." Jarrod Kintz

The whole landscape and nature of relationships in the western world is being revolutionised and transformed, the once traditional views are being thrown out the window and common views are being smashed, some for the better and some for the worse.

The emergence of technology and social media is changing the game we play, the new generation of young males and females lack a confidence and personality like no age before them, they shun conventional communication methods in favour of impersonal, shallow substance less pursuits, gone are the days of meeting someone face to face, sharing a conversation exchanging telephone numbers and catching up for a meal or drink, gone is the need for confidence, good talk, wit and personality.

The youngsters of today much rather the abundance of social media platforms like Facebook, Plenty of Fish, Skout, Blender, Instagram and many more to woo one another with shallow and ego filled instant messages, posts, comments and pictures. You don't approach someone who catches your eye with pure confidence and guts; you get their name from a friend and send them a message. This raises the question, is this new technology breeding a culture of scared little boys?

People seem to be in such a rush to find someone, due to constant pressures from peers and the media that they enter relationships based on nothing, this meaningless new
45

age fluff and more often than not this initial lack of confidence displayed by both parties leads to unhealthy, unhappy relationships, in which they both stay in due to their lack of ability to find anybody else. The constant pressure and stigma that you should be with someone at a certain age rings loud in the ears of many, ask a single man or lady at the age of 28 or above how many times someone older than them has asked them why they don't have a girlfriend or boyfriend or why they aren't married and the response will be very high.

 People are then happy to conform to these expectations when they meet their first suitable match, they then settle for a life of mediocrity as a result. Not knowing that the people with these expectations come from a different world to today, they were married at twenty two, had eight kids and worked every day for sixty years, that was their life, people were born to breed and that was it, the world has changed and conforming to these out dated ignorant views will cost you dearly.

These out dated views and expectations are the reason why divorce rates in the western world are at a record high and that in a time of economic and social prosperity people still suffer from crippling unhappiness.

Marriage falls right into this category of gone with the times, out dated and potentially redundant. Up until recent times marriage has been the fundamental stepping stone for every relationship but does it still carry the same aura and status as yesteryear. People are shunning marriage and the massive costs that go with it in record numbers, believing staying in committed unmarried relationships has no difference. Couples are having kids out of wedlock without the once heavy stigma attached, claiming it demonstrates a show of commitment greater than any marriage certificate will ever convey and rightly so.

It saddens me to see a couple somewhat just going through the steps, the routine, well we've been together for five years the logical next stage is to get married. Well is it, last time I checked it wasn't 1984. More focus should be placed on ridding yourselves of any social expectations and doing what is best for each individual, rushing into these arrangements will only add to the already damming divorce figures.

With these changes in the traditional dating scene come with it many dangers. Our children are developing without the fundamental tools needed for a happy, healthy life. They are replacing the basic qualities of communication, personality and confidence with shy, nervous, reclusiveness. It is only a matter of time before too much T.V and Facebook and lack of any real face to face relationships will foster lifelong habits detrimental to their health.

When I turned eighteen my older brother handed me a book called 'The Game' written by Neil Strauss and told me if you're going to spend a lot of your time chasing girls then you may as well be good at it. You might question that this method is unhealthy and dangerous, but anything that can encourage a young man, battling with confidence and shyness especially with the opposite sex to communicate and socialise with girls is a good thing. A very good thing, it meant meeting new people, learning different personality traits, it created new relationships and friendships and dramatically developed confidence and self- esteem.

I fear that the new age of 'picking up' and 'dating' online and via mobile applications will mean young boys will not gain any of these benefits and it will lead to a whole bunch of insecure boys and girls too afraid and nervous to truly express themselves and therefore getting into relationships for all the wrong reasons and in turn missing out on experiencing a whole world of opportunities and splendid adventures.

I think that it is absolutely vital that young people experience a whole range of things in all areas and that is especially important when it comes to developing and fostering relationships with the opposite sex. How can one know he has found the 'right' person or a good match if they haven't first tested the waters so to speak? This doesn't mean dating numerous girls at once; having many ongoing sexual flings, reaching the century milestones and collecting flags the world over, but it's definitely a good start. The simple fact is the more you experience the better idea you have of what you want; this goes for all things in life; girls, sex, relationships and marriage included.

Sex is a contentious topic; it always has been and always will be. Girls and sex have been arguably two of my biggest vices. They have been the reason for many failures, many mistakes and constant confusion, but for some reason, the desires within when not controlled continue to wreak havoc.

As young teenagers in school and sporting teams pressure is put on young men about whether they have been with a girl, did they get to first base, have you got a girl etc. this talk and constant debate is the reason why sex is placed so high in young kids minds and they get this unreal, disillusioned view of what it actually is, it is placed on this imaginary pedestal and thought of this great achievement which leads to years and decades of chasing after this fantasy like mecca.

When we are young we love to follow the crowd and do
48

the cool 'in' thing, at the top of this list is sex. With all this hype and social pressures to conform there are some dangers that are lurking and no 'birds and bees' speech can prepare the youth for it, nor can getting students throwing condoms on bananas in school, we need to be real because it's a real world out there and real mistakes happen.

It's all this hype mixed with ill-informed education that causes issues and I am not talking about sexually transmitted diseases or unwanted pregnancies, these are all well documented, I am talking about the creation of sex and ego, having sex to tell the mates, to get status, to get numbers on the board, to show pictures to the boys, to treat girls like objects. This is all too common and with the introduction and boom of social media and online dating this is going crazy. These days you don't even have to talk to a girl to have sex with them, just send a photo or a message and meet up via the almost endless media platforms.

These platforms are blurring the lines between right and wrong with privacy out the window. It's giving these insecure, shy and nervous kids direct access to the girls that they crave so much but couldn't previously attain and I don't think we realise the dangers that this presents.

Sex is made out to be this big deal, it's talked about in schools as this ultimate prize, its everywhere we look in the media, on TV, splashed across glossy magazines, on billboards, in movies and it has created this unnecessary aura that pressures young children and it's the ego that causes the most issues.

A lot of the time I went home with girls, not because I liked them or because they were interesting or good looking but because I wanted the boys to see me pick them up, I wanted them to ask me the next day, I wanted them to tell everyone how they saw me take her home, in other words I wanted and needed them to inflate my ego. I started going home with girls I knew I didn't like just because it was the end of the night and as the boys put it 'a roots a root' and truth be told I couldn't wait to tell everyone what I did to her the next day. You hear stories from older mates about how they went travelling and got twenty flags, twenty girls from twenty different countries and this drives you for more. This usually involves drunken one night stands, drunken phone calls or boring Tuesday nights with nothing to do, so you use girls to satisfy this desire that you've been bombarded with all your life.

You might argue what's wrong with this, the girls are consensual adults, but the bigger problem is it is the start of a very bad habit that is difficult to stop, you keep on throwing logs on the fire and the flames just get bigger, it starts to kill your time and I can't tell you how much time I've wasted trying to pick up girls just because she has amazing breasts or because I heard she's great in bed, it becomes the reason why you go out every weekend and you are lucky if you come out the other end of this addiction with any sort of sanity.

There is a massive direct link between sex, alcohol and drugs. It is only after I have had a big break from endless drinking and drug benders that my intense cravings for sex and girls dissolve. But when I am drinking and heading out continuously, sex is constantly on my mind, Monday to Friday, leading to some terrible decision making, followed by some more terrible decision making, it is only when this major force of alcohol is restricted that you get this clarity that allows you to see things a little clearer. When you are drinking you are out and about, heading to pubs and parties where you are surrounded by plenty of ladies, add

50

to this you are with the boys so energy and banter are high and inhibitions twisted. All the talk, the music and the short skirts activate the mind and the last ten years of programming means there's only one thing on your mind. And this is where the other dangers bear there evil head.

I have a few mates who pay for their drunken nights and will pay forever, not just financially which is a massive, substantial on- going burden, but emotionally, which weighs you down just as much. One night, extremely intoxicated, no memory stands that lead to the dreaded pregnancy. This is not uncommon; in fact it's all too common; many have escaped this scot free, a little scare here and there but life goes on. But unfortunately for some they were not so lucky, we all have mates that don't wear condoms, either by being too drunk or not caring, but is absolutely necessary and paramount that you always insist on throwing one on especially on a one night stand. No practicing putting one on a banana in year ten will prepare you for when you are fifteen drinks deep, 2am, semi naked with a naked lady in front of you in all her glory with the hormones pumping and a few other things.

It is a tough enough job raising a child in an environment with great support networks of mother and father, but to throw that burden on just the mother with just the financial support from a stranger is another thing. It's a tough pill to swallow for a guy who seemingly is just having a bit of fun like everyone around him, now has to pay money month to month for a child he had with a stranger that he can barely remember and that's the least of the issues, what about the child's well- being?

What about Chlamydia, herpes and syphilis and warts and other crazy sexually transmitted diseases, because we all know somebody who has these or has had these and they

51

aren't pretty.

So don't leave the education of sex and pregnancy to some lame 'birds and bees' fable or to an equally lame PE unit in school, drum in the reality and all its consequences and make young people really think whether it's worth it, because a lot of the time it isn't and even most of time it isn't.

It's common seeing people who act like they have a split personality, one for their friends and then one for their partner. They have this almost separate life where everything about them changes. I'm not talking about letting your hair down and running wild/going out with your friends every now and then because that is fine, I am talking about their partners never seeing different sides to them at all and how they attempt to continually keep it that way.

If you are going to spend a lot of time with someone it is fundamentally important that you are first off good mates, if you are going to spend every day together then it's a downright necessity.

Like in the Friends and Brothers chapter to follow when you have a good mate, you have unbridled honesty, genuinity and authenticity. They are not afraid to hurt your feelings and step on your toes for the betterment of you, they will hit you with the truth no matter how dangerous, they will kick you up the bum when you are lazy and slap you on the back when you're doing well and this is exactly what we should have in our relationships with our girlfriends, boyfriends, husbands and wives.

Great friends make it hard for us to lie to ourselves and cheat ourselves because they see right through our fear and the real reason in why we are acting. Great friends
52

motivate you and inspire you; they embarrass you and know exactly how to pull your strings.

If you keep this other side and secrets to yourself you miss out on this unbridled honesty and authenticity and whole lot of fun and good times. Why do we need this in our mates from the same sex but then not in our marriages or relationships? Do we simply conform to the demands of society and get married by a certain age? Are we happy to settle? Is this why the divorce rate is at a record high? What about the increased rates of domestic violence? Why?

The topic of sex, girls, marriage and relationships could easily fill 20 million books and there are already so many books written on this topic and there will continue to be. Each paragraph of this chapter could easily be expanded to flow over several more pages because it is a topic that consumes our every days, it is everywhere we look, depicted in every T.V show and on every ad we see, it will continue to be a cornerstone of society for ever and it will be a topic of much heated debate for centuries.

What affect technology will have on our lives and this area in particular nobody knows, but I am definitely extremely apprehensive if today's trends are anything to go by. I can only hope that my kids will actually still talk to people face to face, know real communication and know real people.

Health & Happiness

"I promise you nothing is as chaotic as it seems. Nothing is worth your health. Nothing is worth poisoning yourself into stress, anxiety, and fear." Steve Maraboli

Without good health you simply cannot enjoy the joys of life, so with that in mind, health has to be the most important thing in life. But why is it that our health repeatedly takes the backseat to the focus and pursuit of big houses and fast cars? Why is working that twelve hour day at the top of our priority list day in day out? Is stress normal? Are we all living for tomorrow instead of today?

I have always lived a life of excess and extremes, plenty of beers, plenty of food, lots of work, plenty of treating the body and mind with total disdain and disrespect. But everything we do now has a direct link and impact on all of our tomorrows, and maybe it is only now that I'm truly realising this.

I had an epiphany not too long ago, it involved the loss of hair and what appeared to be my imminent balding, the effects of ten years or so of this unruly disrespect. It was my first real wakeup call that I was getting older and in fact uglier probably also less smart and the one thing that is normally synonymous with age, wisdom; wasn't exactly growing either. I decided to go on my usual yearly detox of good food and plenty of exercise, where I aim to replenish my body after months on end of binge drinking. So I get into 'binge' detoxing, (makes sense and very healthy too!) Instead I started to find what has usually worked so well wasn't going so smoothly. My body had finally caught up with itself, my usual long runs where hindered by the
54

introduction of knee pain and when I struggled to do the incredibly difficult ten pushups, I thought to myself that maybe my philosophy of extremism might be better served with a big touch of balance.

We seem to live in an age of information, progress and growth and a somewhat unfounded faith in science and technology. When it comes to our own health and wellbeing and the question of choice, the options seem endless. Our profit driven society thrives on the introduction of new fads, fashions, and gimmicks and corporations seem to spend just as much time turning natural things like growing old into chronic illnesses that they can fix – for a price.

It is not hard for a wealthy company to fund research that will turn results very much in favour of their product, making it easy to sway social ideals and create a product that becomes a huge cash crop, only giving them more power and influence to create more confusion for them to exploit.

Eat 'real' food. What is 'real' food?

It's a sign of the times that I'm even answering this question. Forget fancy labels – Low fat, sugar free, non-genetically modified, glycemic index, Natural colours, Flavours etc… Forget well placed advertisements and big budgets creating food fashions that are cheap and devoid of anything nourishing. Think real food that grows, ripens and rots. Spend your precious time digging it up and not standing around reading the coercive label thought up by a well-paid consumer psychologist, who wants to sell at the cost of your health. Think raw and organic later, for now just fill your body with real food and see how you feel.

Scribbles on the Wall: Lessons Along the Way

Spend more time with 'real' people.

I don't care how many 'friends' you have on face book, or how many movies or sitcoms you can recite verbatim! Or that you've had the same friends since kindergarten! The research says if you want to be happy and healthy, spend time with 'real' people and do real things – connect with groups and grow. Go for a walk, talk, do a dance, sing a bloody song, argue, just get away from the computer and the television they are not the healthy option!

Move everything – everyday.

Forget fancy gym routines, cross fit circuits and drill sergeant sessions in the park – just move! Once again it's a sign of the times, when people regularly speed off in the car, past the un-cut grass and hedge, spend 8 minutes finding a spot close to the entrance, do the shopping 2 minutes down the road, so they can hurry down to the gym and jog on an electric treadmill for 1 hour in the luxury of their air conditioned gym. The sun, the trees, the grass, the sand, all traded for the hype and an expensive monthly payment – I hope your biceps are worth it! And for the folks that live in the big cities – whatever, just move.

Do the things you love – often.

Forget giving things up, instead take things up! Don't quit – get involved!

Do nothing – everyday.

Obesity is becoming common place amongst young as well as old. But our relationship to doing is chronic and this is reflected in our stress and anxiety. Too much worrying and planning for the future is rarely remedied by telling people to not worry. Even if the advice makes sense, in practice it is almost impossible to give up such an old habit. Take time each day to relax (not in front of the television, or drink a beer or eat food – do nothing). Pull yourself together and just 'stop'. Watch the children sleep, the waves roll in, the trees blowing in the breeze or whatever it is – but just be present for a moment and be gracious for the opportunity you have. Life is not measured by how much you have done, how fast you ran or how high you jumped. Maybe it is measured by how often you smiled and laughed – stopping is a time to enjoy.

Good health is contagious, so do as Gandhi said and 'be the change you want to see in the world' Happiness and wealth grow from good health – so forget the big corporations' cons and get healthy.

Everything in life is inter- related, dependent on one thing or another, everything is intrinsically linked through unseen bounds and nothing is impacted more than a pull or a push here or there then our health. Our health is the cornerstone of life, too much of an extreme in alcohol or work or diet will cause a ripple effect down the line impacting directly on one's health.

You might be able to get away with things in other aspects of life, but sooner or later it will inevitably hit you where it counts and that is your health. Too many people consistently perform tasks that are detrimental to their health and the health of others around them, they burn their days doing something they hate, going to that job that saps their time and energy, thinking that it will mean a

57

brighter tomorrow, but each day it crosses off anther tomorrow and that plan of moving up the coast to your dream spot in five more years of work may never come.

We touched on this in the 'work and money' section, but it is worth repeating, when asked what surprised him most about humanity the Dalai Lama said;

"Man, because he sacrifices his health in order to make money.

Then he sacrifices money to recuperate his health.

And then he is so anxious about the future that he does not enjoy the present;

The result being that he does not live in the present or the future;

He lives as if he is never going to die, and then dies having never really lived."

This is all too true, people are falling sick all around us but we still find it necessary to fulfill this somewhat invisible dream, when we all have the ability to live it right now. We get ourselves so deep in debt and distraction that we lose focus on what this all about; or we are all so distracted from birth and the years of programming and pressures that maybe we've had the wrong focus all along.

My brother when on a Yoga and meditation retreat in Europe told me a story of a German man named Jeremy with whom he was living with. Jeremy had stress induced sciatica and has trouble walking and also lying down. He said it is from his father, who he doesn't get along with and has been working with for twenty years. He found his way to the retreat to learn how to deal with stress, but I cannot help to think that this is not the real answer. For too many people go to yoga or meditation when they should be devoting more time to communicating with their loved ones, working smarter, getting more involved in life instead of hiding away from it. Dealing with stress is only a portion of the answer, creating less stress through living within ones means and living well is much more than the other half.

We see it every day on the TV news, in the newspapers that sitting in cars and traffic every day is dangerous and crippling to our health, we see that being unmotivated and uninterested in your daily job is dangerous and crippling to our health, we see that too much alcohol is dangerous and crippling to our health and we see that staying in bad relationships is dangerous and crippling to our health, but why do we do it every day? We could all die tomorrow chasing dreams we don't really know why, living a life where the things we love are a second and third priority.

Ask yourself if you had one year left to live would you do the things you are doing today?

If you died today would you be happy with what you have done and things you have chased after?

Would you be content and satisfied?

Do you know 'why' you do the things you do?

Have you ever asked yourself 'why' you do things?

Sometimes we need more meaning and purpose and sitting back and asking 'why' might just deliver this purpose and meaning you are looking for. We act so fast, running through life that we sometimes forget why we started doing it in the first place; it is absolutely paramount that we take a break to take a deep look at ourselves and discover 'why' we do the things we do so we can enjoy the time we have doing the things we love with the people we love.

We don't need to give up things but just find that good balance, because everything we do comes back to the cornerstone which is health and health means a hell lot more than what you read in your monthly men's health magazine and it means so much more than getting your thirty minutes of exercise each day and how you did a triathlon last week or do a yoga class on Mondays. As some wise person said centuries ago, health is wealth.

But in this age of fads, big egos and too much cool, health needs to be drummed up to have its importance stand out from the crowd and force its way into the twittersphere. Health is working a job that's not really a job because you love it so much you'll get up and do it anyway, it's too much laughter with great mates and family, it's good food that takes more than ten minutes to arrive at your table, or the table is a grass hill overlooking the beach or park, or its log around the campfire, it's a good book you read not to pass a course but because you enjoy it, it's falling off that surfboard more times then you remember but doing just enough so when you finally get it, you want to do it again and again, it's about being surrounded by people who care more about you than they do themselves, it's about waking up each morning in a place you feel safe with endless opportunities, it's about confidence and self-belief, about passion and love. It's not low carbs, protein shakes and the new ab roller 1000; it's not your expensive monthly gym membership and the high paying eighty hour week job or the high rise on the beach. It is clarity, it is contentment and it is freedom.

"Everything that happens in life good or bad happens for a reason, what you take from it determines how good or bad it is"

People see happiness as the end goal, but happiness is the thing that happens when your living life. It's the by-product of everyday, it can't be reached at the end of the day, and then be simply gone the next day. It seems to be what everyone is chasing, what everyone wants. But in the confusion of life, with so much on one's plate it slips further and further down the list of priorities, before you know it you're stuck in the harsh cycle of routine with too much responsibility and too many commitments to stop and think why you actually started doing it in the first place.

When we are young, everything is new and fresh, a simple walk down to the river is an exciting journey that makes us happy, happiness seems so much more attainable, we didn't have much money when I was growing up, that's not to say we didn't have everything we needed, but my memories are filled with fun, and excitement, freedom and happiness.

As we grow older we are shown all these different 'concepts' of what it takes to be a success in life, what we need, how much money we need to earn, what car we should drive, the big house all these material possessions that when attained will deliver happiness.

I am guilty of getting lost in this world of material pleasure, and superficial status. It's a beautiful place, the tall trees and singing birds have been replaced with giant plasmas and fast cars. The days are gone of saving up for something we want, we are under the reign of plastic cards

61

that when the right digits are entered, presto, Instant happiness. We seem to have replaced the most perfect emotion of happiness with the concept material possessions will fulfil our every need.

Science (Positive Psychology) sees these factors as integral in cultivating peace, joy and happiness.

1. Money – We need a certain amount for shelter, food and clothing, above this level people achieve no more happiness.

2. Goals – Enjoyable, meaningful and achievable goals.

3. Mindfulness – The ability to saviour life, enjoy simple pleasures and recognise beauty and enjoy the present moment. People who think a lot and ruminate a lot have lower levels of joy and higher levels of depression and dissatisfaction.

4. Gratitude – Thankful for the conditions you have already. Health, wealth, opportunity, friends, family.

5. Giving – People who hug or volunteer are happier than those who don't. People who give real compliments and support others in time of hardship but even more so when things are going right, have more joy and happiness

6. Exercise – At least thirty minutes a day of cardio exercise

7. Relationships – Support, social contacts, quality of contacts. Friends are more involved in our level of happiness than our spouse.

Evan Sutter

8. Proximity – If you want to be happy, wise, confident, loving etc. then you have to be around these kinds of people. 'Environment'.

Lots of people die from loneliness, caught in isolation when all they have to do is get involved. Cardiovascular disease is also linked to relationships and environment.

Happiness, joy, obesity and depression spread like viruses and too often are culture resorts to band- aid fixes and in many ways they help. Deep or slightly deep alliances and bonds are born over a beer in pubs, friends laugh and share and enjoy being together. People feel sad they enjoy food, if they are lonely they get a DVD and this helps, it relieves and it allows healing, but only for a short time. To be really happy we should practice each of these every day with all our diligence.

Happiness is being totally comfortable with the person we are, happiness comes from taking the time to enjoy the more pure things in our lives, our friendships and our relationships with loved ones. Happiness comes with not living in our pasts, not getting lost in the future but enjoying right now. Happiness and Health is very much the same thing, you can't have one without the other.

Drugs & Alcohol

"I've wanted to feel pleasure to the point of insanity. They call it getting high, because it's wanting to know that higher level, that godlike level. You want to touch the heavens, you want to feel glory and euphoria, but the trick is it takes work. You can't buy it, you can't get it on a street corner, you can't steal it or inject it or shove it up your ass, you have to earn it." Anthony Kiedis

Drugs are such a common occurrence day in day out all over the world these days, the once stigmatised topic is very much mainstream and its risks and dangers have somewhat been replaced by a bigger focus on money, wealth and mortgages. I have had more than my fair share of drugs and I can sit on both sides of the fence when it comes to the good and bad.

Alcohol is so heavily entrenched in western society that it widely occurs in most social events, it seems to have slipped under the radar in terms of the problems it has on individuals and the community at large. There have been few weekends over the last ten years that I and my mates haven't got together; typically including large amounts of beer, spirits and/or drugs.

I have had some pretty fun days on the drink and drugs, some really cool, memorable times all over the world, some of my best memories include being in very inebriated states, so you won't find me telling you to stay away and don't touch anything, I believe it's a learning curve necessary for every young person as they grow up, a very steep curve at times, that can teach you some very harsh lessons, but what I will tell you, is to be aware of what it can do, because as I have learned sometimes these lessons

64

don't give you a second chance.

I have seen people die from car crashes and accidents; people beaten to within a limb of their life, overdoses, people jailed, fined, pregnancies, diseases, near misses and lucky escapes, seen people lose friends and loved ones. You might say these are the extremes, the one offs and these people must have big issues and excessive problems, but no, people are dying from mixing red bulls and vodkas, people staggering out of pubs and getting hit by cars, casual drinkers are getting beaten with glass bottles and king hit, it doesn't mean don't go anywhere, stay inside and live your life on social media, but just be aware.

I have experienced a vast range of substances whether it be in my home town or whilst travelling, whether it be mushrooms in Amsterdam or Cocaine throughout Europe and the U.S; the fact is, this is very common, just social situations, just fun recreational use with friends and for most people I know this is nothing out of the ordinary, but there is a fine line between normality and troubles, and the problem is this fine line can't be seen and it differs for every individual.

The fact is the dangers are plain and clear. You simply do not know what is in the drugs these days. Drug suppliers and drug dealers have no problem adding and mixing any chemicals to their product as long as it improves their bottom line. Ecstasy tablets contain anything from heroin, LSD, rat poison; crushed glass and methamphetamine, veterinary anaesthetics, anything that can 'bulk' up their product and make them more money. Dangerous bulking agents also include the deadly Paramethoxyamphetamine which has been linked to a string of overdoses across Australia and Levamisole a pesticide used to de-worm animals.

Scribbles on the Wall: Lessons Along the Way

Every time you purchase any kind of drug you just don't know what you will be consuming, each time you will get variable potency and variable purity and the potential for permanent brain damage from just single use is very common.

I've had good friends turn from popular, beautiful, gifted teenagers with unlimited potential in to strangers, social outcasts, unable to handle a conversation, trapped in their minds and prisoners of their own cravings with no friends and no dreams.

Few have managed to turn things around through hard work and great discipline the others haven't been so lucky. The days of finding work and earning independent living are sadly behind them and the saddest part is these where normal guys, no different to anyone else our age, just either there body couldn't handle it or their mind couldn't let them stop.

They now mix their time between incarceration, depression, mental homes and reclusiveness. Their lives have changed forever, as it has for their families and closest loved ones, who have to see these changes and have to watch as their beloved spiral further and further out of control, feeling helpless and guilt stricken and it seems any chance of normality has blown away just like the smoke once did from their bottle.

These are just some of the results, whilst quite heavy and shocking; they can happen to anyone, maybe luck has been on my mates and my side. Not too long ago a mate was set upon by a group of cowards and beaten to a pulp as he walked out of the pub down the road to the taxi, he was both unlucky, wrong place wrong time, but lucky, he is alive and healthy now, he only had six beers and was relatively in a good state at the time, Not long before I had a few mates come home after a big night on the drink, try some of their sick mates morphine, only to get a bad reaction and fall unconscious and be lucky to survive.

Me and an old roommate took a few stillnox tablets one afternoon with a few beers, just two guys having a little fun, next minute we are driving three hours out of town to a friend's place, according to her on arrival we were incoherent and on "another planet" the next morning we had no memory of the night before except for a few strange recounts from friends and the car parked five metres off the driveway.

This is just a simple example of how drugs and alcohol, whether it is the well- known dangerous drugs or the harmless accepted ones, can be extremely dangerous when you are not aware. What if we crashed into a young family, what if we hit a pole, we couldn't see much and can't recall anything, so we were very lucky to even wake up the next day, not in a prison cell or not in a morgue. We think we were most likely sleep walking, but one thing is for certain and that is we were definitely very stupid.

Being intoxicated or under the effect of drugs can put you in places a sober 'sane' you would never find yourself in, simply because you will say yes to things you would normally say no and you will hang out with people you normally think are fools. This could mean a cool after weisen party (after Oktoberfest party in Munich) a girl's house in Lisbon, a random surf trip down the coast of Portugal, but it could also mean something completely different.

Let me paint you a picture and you be the judge. First night in New Orleans, USA, extremely intoxicated, extremely is some understatement, a friend and I enjoying the epic music and the abundance of easy going happy people in the many bars lining Bourbon Street. Blissfully unaware of the potential dangers the area possesses, especially out of the main tourist hub, where poverty, crime and anarchy run wild, the two of us accept a lift home with a young attractive girl who has caught our interest. Next minute, in what we know now is a common practise amongst the locals, the car pulls up and we jump out and we are encountered by some rather large African American men, who then demand money, the ensuing chase involves leaping many fences as bullets fly past our heads, we manage to avoid death and hide out in a nearby McDonalds restaurant whilst waiting for the police to arrive, they never did, they were too busy answering to the many actual murders that occurred that night. If we weren't in such a poor, inebriated state, we could have seen right through the situation, that the girl had targeted us for a robbery, we were lucky to get away to tell the story, many people are not. You can still have fun and have great times and not be so written off that you fall prey to the wickedness of others.

I have been out most weekends for over ten years and so have most of my mates, out to clubs or pubs, to parties, to weddings, birthdays, and work events, I've been so drunk on many occasions that I can't remember a single thing, not one thing from eight hours, it makes you wonder who you were with, what you were saying, how you were acting, where you went.

 It opens up a window of time where anything could have happened to you where you would have little or no control over. Not only this it makes you wonder what people perceptions would be of you, I could have been carrying on like an absolute idiot and chances are in that state I probably was. One thing for certain is its not only me, this happens to almost all my mates. Some of who will have to pay for their drunkenness forever with child support payments from one night stands that they hardly remember. Raising the question; why? Why subject yourself to this and what about all this wasted time?

When you laugh and when you have sex your body releases serotonin, this allows you to feel amazing, each time you take drugs the serotonin takes a back seat to the artificial high being exerted from the drugs. That's why the next day it's common to feel lonely and depressed as the serotonin builds itself up after not being called upon, take drugs continuously over a period of time and the serotonin levels become almost non- existent and that could be exactly why depression is so prevalent.

It's such common social practise in the western world that you have a few beers or a few wines, it occurs at weddings and funerals at work parties and just about everything in between, it is difficult to avoid it, it's tough to say no to a drink especially when it's been programmed in your social conditioning all your life that doing so is the norm, it's what Dad and the Uncles did at Christmas and it has been passed down from generation to generation. It's how we celebrate, how we relax, how we enjoy, how we mourn and how we communicate. We somehow find it ok to spend the days that follow miserable, tired and sick, wasting time and opportunities.

I realise I have wasted a lot of time, too many days in bed, sick, not being able to move, recovering from the tolls of the days and nights before, I have said to myself endless times, "why" and "never again" but it keeps dragging us back in. Are our lives that miserable that billions of people around the world find the need to get extremely intoxicated day in day out or do we just love hanging out with friends and this is how we do it?

Scribbles on the Wall: Lessons Along the Way

These are all relatively short term consequences, what the future has in store after years of destroying, disrespecting and diluting the body and mind is another thing.

What about the missed opportunities that you will never get back from the wasted time and focus? Not being ready to pounce when opportunity presented itself.

What about financially? Wow. Yes, I have had some great times, but when you think about how much it has cost you in your pocket, you really have to wonder was it worth it. $300 a night on beers and spirits and whatever else may join the party, week in week out, throw in the Monday sickies, the day after eat outs and it could be that new house you've always wanted.

I write this standing at the end of my drugs and alcohol experiences, well at least the end of the 4 day benders, black outs, lack of control and stupid decisions. I consider myself lucky to have experienced some absolutely amazing times influenced by their work and luckier to have largely forgone the dangers and consequences apart from the odd broken nose, lost friendship and damaged ego.

Yes there are dangers associated with drugs and alcohol and sometimes these dangers have nothing to do with how responsible and how careful you are but we as individuals need to surround ourselves with good people, good friends and family to be there for support, an extra eye and ear and for criticism and judgement when we need it, so we can all experience life and take our own lessons from it.

We need to all find the balance in what we do, with work, family and especially drugs and alcohol, anything done to the extreme will sooner or later cause big issues, we need to strike a balance that is good for you as an individual and one which allows you to still live happily moving forward doing the things you love and not effecting the ones you love.

And we need to ask ourselves 'why', a simple 'why am I doing this' before a lot of things in life will stop a lot of unnecessary hurt and bring great light into what you're actually doing.

Religion & Faith

"My religion is very simple. My religion is kindness." Dalai Lama XIV

Why is it that we live in a time far more advanced and far more educated and religion still seems to determine the way millions live their lives. Religions have become mainstream, a trend almost, everywhere I look kids seem to be attaching themselves to religions. I have no animosity or feel no prejudice towards anyone who believes in religion or gods as long as they know why they choose to spend their time on earth worshipping gods in the sky.

Instead of teaching our future generations that we create our own hope and that we create our own luck we teach them to pray to gods in the sky and ask for help. Surely teaching children communication skills and importance of confidence and discipline amongst many others are a higher priority than something that lacks relevance in today's world.

I would rather my nieces and nephews develop their own set of values and ethics through experience and their own life rather than the principles from thousands of years ago. More so than this, I want them to learn that if they want something in life then only they can get it, not through praying before bed each night to someone else but through hard work, commitment, trial and error and discipline. They need to understand to put the faith, belief and trust in themselves and that no one else is going to do it for them.

We need to emphasize to the young people we love that life is short and the great importance in living it to the fullest by chasing your dreams and doing the things you love, we can't afford to drum into them that there's this great land where you go after you die which is perfect, but instead we need to focus on the harsh reality of the world today; this will hold them in better stead moving forward as they grow and develop.

Religion and finding your faith in the world is a great thing if you are an adult who has experienced life and has walked many a path. Coming to this place from your own accord and own actions for the belief that it makes you a better person and sharing it with other like- minded individuals and a community you respect, feel safe in and enjoy is a great thing. But is pushing different belief systems and rules on young under- developed minds the right thing to do? Are we better off letting are young people experience their own path and in turn make their own decisions?

I was walking over a bridge in Las Vegas in the U.S.A and there was a young boy no older than eight years old. He stood on a bridge in a popular pedestrian walkway and yelled into a microphone about God and the Devil and Sinners. His father stood just metres away to the side; just far enough to avoid the spotlight but close enough to continually subtly bark instructions to his son. Was this healthy for this young boy to be burdened with such a great load of information? It was plain to see for anybody passing through that night no matter what nationality or background that this young boy was brainwashed and forced to suffer a pain that he will undoubtedly have to face somewhere down the track. Putting your child through this is a heavy burden to carry, he might not be preaching in public on a microphone but is the load he carries any lighter?

73

Unloading such heavy information on an under developed mind is very overwhelming and can be very dangerous. Instead of providing a range of information on a range of areas and allowing our children to develop at their own pace and come to their own outcomes, we feed them our own specific beliefs and nothing else. At such a young age they are inadvertently taught that what they believe is 'right' and the others 'wrong' with no common ground, subsequently drawing these dangerous labels and unnecessary segregation.

Everyone is entitled to their set of beliefs and values but not everyone is entitled to preach these words and beliefs to everyone. I heard a great analogy for what I'm trying to say and I think it went a little bit like this. 'It's great to have a penis and be proud of it, but don't go waving it around in public and definitely don't go throwing it down my children's throat', I think this is very much the same for religion, yes, stay strong with your beliefs and If they work for you then even better, but no need to hammer down the throats of anyone who will listen, if the word is as grand as you speak, then people will find it eventually.

I still find it a little strange that a book written thousands of years ago can hold so much power and relevance in the modern world especially in a world with a plethora of technology pleasing everyone's need for fast fixes and shallow, materialistic obsession. Maybe that is one thing that makes religions and the like so strong thousands of years after their creation and that is people's desire for fast and easy fixes, forget working for something, sit back and pray that someone else can help; sound familiar?

Many religions have some great foundations built on for example respect for thy neighbor, but for the better development of our children and future generations these

74

are the things that should be learnt at home and amongst friends not from an ancient book written by someone they don't know. These real life examples and demonstrations will resonate with them more than any book, fictitious or real. We shouldn't let the foundations of our children's lives be built by strangers but instead by us, us as leaders and positive role models, we should be the Jesus or Allah in our kid's lives.

It is wonderful to witness people overcome massive hurdles in their life and make drastic changes and a lot of the times it is through what they describe as 'finding God'. But despite the development and progress they have made is it only a temporary façade to mask over their problems of the past; instead of making these changes internally they just manage to paint over the issues by picking up something else to dull them while never actually fixing it to start with.

I have seen people all of sudden turn into born again Christians and decide to now abstain from sex before marriage, when I have asked why I haven't been able to detect a clear reasoning, I feel that it is just another way of covering up another underlying issue. I have no problem whatsoever with any choice a person makes that they believe is for the betterment of them and has no effect on anyone else, but I do have to question it especially when it occurs to young people who have enough trouble deciding on what to wear let alone cope with straining external pressures and prejudices.

Young people have enough on their plate as it is with so many pressures facing them from peers and unrealistic social expectations to have to be faced with another one which carries with it so much heated debate, let them find what they find in their own time without any pressure or push from anyone. We need to encourage individualism and uniqueness and create a platform for where forging your own path and own decisions are cultivated.

Religion today is a business and a big business at that and like any business they are run for profit and revenue and like any business we sometimes need to sit back and question their motives. I don't think religion is the answer for fragile minds and people in poor state of minds, because this acts as a cover up and a very light façade and I don't think it is the place for young people who have under developed minds and all too much confusion as it is.

Religion shouldn't hire highly paid advertising executives to drive bigger crowds to their denomination; it shouldn't be concerned with having consumer psychologists on board in order to entice and sell their product; because then is it any better than the packaging on cigarettes or alcohol sponsorship?

Religion is not what it once was, it's now more a business than anything else competing in a very cluttered market trying to get an advantage anyway it can, and that is a dangerous game to be involved in. From what was born out of simple values is now a fashion and a fad, it is a label for young teens to aspire to.

While society is endeavoring to break down walls and bring cultures together religion manages to keep on putting them up and pushing people apart as it has for centuries and centuries.

Ask yourself would the world be better without religion, the reason for the start of most wars, fighting and prejudices in the history of mankind?

Friends

"Friendship is the hardest thing in the world to explain. It's not something you learn in school. But if you haven't learned the meaning of friendship, you really haven't learned anything." Muhammad Ali

I believe that one of the most important things in life if not the most important thing is surrounding yourself with good people. If you surround yourself with good people then you open yourself up to all of life's beauties.

Over a period of life we gain and lose friends, people come and go, some naturally through time and some through unsavoury happenings, it isn't a bad thing, it doesn't warrant over thinking and getting emotional it is simply a part of life, how you adapt and respond makes all the difference.

Friends are going to deceive you, they are going to tell lies and talk rubbish, and they are going to try to bring you down in order to make them look good and inflate their own egos and sense of self-worth. This is all too common but don't let it affect you, brush it off, brush them and get on with it.

Just recently I had a good mate who I had known for over fifteen years make up lies and stories about me to another friend as if he was still in school looking to make friends and look cool, I could have got upset, gave him a call and yelled abuse. I could have put one on his chin next time I saw him, but instead I was happy, happy too just let him go and not waste any more of my time kicking around with him. (Saving $50 on his next present too).

Scribbles on the Wall: Lessons Along the Way

We are always going to come across people more interested in what others think of them and who go out of their ways in order to get their acceptance and pats on their back; this is exactly what this guy was after, he was after a laugh and boost of his own ego and confidence more so than anything else, which is fine when you are sixteen, its common place in every school ground on the planet, young kids, with low self- esteem, no substance and unique character that they endeavour for nothing less than social acceptance at any cost. But don't get angry or offended, laugh, because this is typical of a person who feels the need for identity, no matter how shallow and lame; and the sad part is he will probably go through life searching for others acceptance in everything he does, satisfying others and neglecting that which is most important to him, realising all too late that no one really cared anyway.

When you have a good mate, you have unbridled honesty, genuinity and authenticity. When you are carrying on like an absolute idiot (which will be a lot over the years) they will tell you, they are not afraid to hurt your feelings and step on your toes for the betterment of you, they will hit you with the truth no matter how dangerous, they will kick you up the bum when you are lazy and slap you on the back when you're doing well. They will heap praise on you not hidden behind metaphors or similes to avoid embarrassment, they will come out clean with it. They will also annoy you, make you upset and angry, hurt your feelings because everything they are saying is the truth and sometimes the last thing we want to hear is the truth.

Great friends make it hard for us to lie to ourselves and cheat ourselves because they see right through our fear and the real reason in why we are acting. Great friends motivate you and inspire you; they embarrass you and

78

know exactly how to pull your strings. Great friends are what we think of when we think of great memories and great friends make what Christopher McCandless said in the movie and book 'Into the Wild' "Happiness is only real when shared" very, very true.

I have one big regret in my life and it involves what I describe above; a 'great' friend. Great friends are there for each other when we need them most, in those moments in life when things turn to their worst no matter the time or the place; you drop everything and get there and in that time when my brother needed me most I wasn't there. Five years have passed and the feeling hasn't changed, when you let down someone you love, someone and something that is real, it burns deep.

If I had my time over I would have jumped on that plane, five or six planes no matter how many it took and I would have travelled across the world to be there, it's funny how you think of the money or how much time it will take, but one thing it teaches you is the money you will get back but that time you never will. I fear that what we once had will never be again, when that trust and faith you have in someone disappears even for a second it's a tough thing to get back. You can carry on thinking that all is fine and everything is back to normal but you can never really fill in that gaping hole in time.

You need great friends and brothers to be a priority in your life, too often we let our desires for money and status get in the way, we are far too busy with our own lives chasing after largely material insignificant objects that we let the real things that matter sit by the wayside.

We are too consumed by these objects of status and prestige that we don't nourish these vitally important relationships, we are in too much of a hurry to pick up the
79

phone or knock on the door, too busy to lift our heads and say g'day and we don't even know how are friends are 'really' doing, we confuse stress for busyness and anger for part of life. We need to cultivate great friendships and forget the new age social media but get real and outside and enjoy the company of the people we love.

I am lucky that I grew up with three older brothers who taught me firsthand what great friends are supposed to be like, who taught me about honesty and integrity and being real and yourself. Who got me outside and into every sport or activity you can think of, who got me into endless trouble, gave me stitches and broken bones. These brothers are the reason why I have an abundance of great friends today because they demonstrated to me what makes a good person and the kind of people that I wanted to surround myself with.

With the plethora of social media platforms today the depth and strength of friendships and relationships in general are being tested, the streets that were once buzzing each afternoon with skateboarders and impromptu games of cricket and football are now replaced with games of PlayStation and Xbox, the saddest part is the games that once included a big group of kids from all ages and backgrounds breeding friendships and trust are cannibalised by kids playing by themselves and breeding reclusiveness and insecurity.

Is the age of 'great friendships' and 'brotherhood' dying? Is the next generation finding their identity through fictional characters on T.V rather than their next door neighbour or class mate?

When I look back on the best times of my life it's the simple things that consistently pop up and they always involve my friends and family. You can have wild parties together with strangers at pool parties in Vegas but you remember the next morning super hung over struggling to eat brekky with your mate. Yeah the Yankees game was pretty cool but it's the 1am walk to little Italy to grab a late night feed with the boys that stands out. You can all go home with beautiful girls after the club but it's kicking with all the boys back at the hotel later that makes you laugh.

It's the early morning coffees and paper with the brother that makes you smile more so than the good surf you had before it; get yourself a good crew of good people to hang around with and you are ensured so many good times, so many laughs and an endless array of amazing memories to pick you up when you are down.

At my Grandfathers 90th Birthday he had friends present who he had known for over seventy years, friends from all corners of the planet, friendships that had endured complete lifetimes, children and grandchildren and life and death and they always maintained contact and shared their incredible lives together whenever they could.

They may not have been the richest men when it came to money but let me tell you from looking around the room that day they were definitely the richest when it came to love, respect and family. This is what real friendships should be like, an entire lifetime of being there for one another and getting through the tough times together; and just imagine the stories they would have to tell.

That day I saw the glow in their eyes when they spoke of the past and when they spoke of each other and I said to myself that day, that this is how I want to be judged, forget money and material objects; it's no point having that if no one can bother to come share your birthdays with you, if no one respects you and can say that you are a great friend and a great person.

Scribbles on the Wall: Lessons Along the Way

As I sat in the doctor's waiting room with my Grandparents I saw firsthand this great need to have great friends and family around. Who is going to take you to the doctors if you get sick and look after you when you are unwell? It saddened me to see some elderly people by themselves, struggling to walk in the door and get up off the seat; and this was only a small part of the struggles they would face in everyday life. But there was my Pop, who had his grandson drop him off at the door and his daughter walk him inside whilst he found a car park, who had someone to talk to as he sat and waited, someone to help him grab the medication from the chemist and just great overall support. There were people aged in their late eighties accompanied by their mates and brothers, helping each other out and sharing in life's many adventures together.

Forget how many friends you have on Facebook or how many followers you have on Twitter, think how many real friends you have that you can be real with, who you can catch up with on your 90th birthday and share a good laugh with and that is what counts.

Life makes it difficult to stay in contact with everyone, but it would be a tragedy to not stay in contact with someone you love. Whip out that phone and drop that text message, Facebook message, tweet, email or update your LinkedIn profile and get in contact with your great friends who are in fact your brothers and organise that get together, learn to laugh again, to smile and get connected how we should and that's face to face.

Spirituality & Enlightened Anarchy

Spirituality

"If a man is to live, he must be all alive, body, soul, mind, heart, spirit." Thomas Merton

I am a human being, with no special talents that I know of, I make mistakes; I forget and remember, often when it is too late. At points in my life, I thought I had the answers and later on I found out that I was simply wrong. It seemed that my latest understandings were just new misunderstandings.

I am simply not sure anymore, which is a kind of relief, for much of my life I thought I had the answers and happily imposed them upon others. I say this for many reasons, firstly because it is true and secondly because when I experienced this simple truth I finally saw myself with a clarity that allowed me to stop pretending. You see, the true spiritual path is not as complex as it may first appear. The many books, practices and institutions that uphold this suspiciously lofty topic, often describe various points along a spectrum that is as long as time and just as illusory. I started out upon the journey for a simple reason, I had done what I was meant to do and it didn't seem to work.

By not working I mean several things. I see these characteristics in many of my peers and it is becoming especially common in young men and women in the west. Especially in societies that have all the so-called perks of modernity. I am talking about isolation, depression, anxiety

83

and a life that ultimately seems meaningless.

As well as great technological advancements, we have created chronic worry and stress, we battle against our bodies trying to keep them young and as a population group it seems we are sicker than ever before. So often I felt the need to tough it out, to be a man and work through my pain, but emotional starvation is a difficult problem for our society to diagnose and amongst the many ways to healing; ignorance and denial were simply not options.

You see for me spirituality is quite simple; it is working patiently and wisely toward order seeing clearly when we are fooling ourselves. From short term pleasure seeking to real happiness, from overwhelming desires to peaceful choices, from isolation to a deep connection to life and a sense of belonging. It is us, discovering that away from the corporation's mistruths about us needing things, we have so much already - in abundance. We simply fail to see the miracle that is present in every moment, we are ignorant and we get along faking it. Although, in this case you cannot fake it till you make it. If you fake it, you simply do not make it.

Corporations survive by overwhelming us with contradictory, one-sided information. Institutions scare us into believing or else and we are pushed and prodded from every angle and as a result we have become idle and when we do act it is not from our best intentions, from our deepest aspiration, it is from a body and mind that is tired and fearful, a body and mind that needs rest and healing.

Chogyam Trungpa once said "Walking the spiritual path properly is a very subtle process; it is not something to jump into naively."

84

There are numerous side-tracks which lead to a distorted, ego, self-centred version of spirituality; we can deceive ourselves into thinking we are progressing spiritually when instead we are strengthening our egocentric self - centeredness through spiritual techniques.

This happens most often when we become attached to concepts and ideals. "Oh, I am a Buddhist now, I do not eat meat, or I am a Christian, I do not judge others." The clothes of a priest, monk or nun, the colours of a yogi, the church and what it represents, the bible and the freedom it promises, these are very little if we do not come to our own heart and begin to really see the truth of each situation.

The first step is seeing that something is simply not working. "I am a Yogi now, but still can't get along with those judgemental lay abouts at work." When I fail to speak honestly, when I hurt others, when I am disrespectful or when I feel insecure, this is the feeling, the fact, this is you. We must be honest and courageous enough to recognise our self-centredness, suffering and fear, to see ourselves simply as we are; that is a good beginning.

A good sign that we are seeing ourselves clearly is that we see how often we exaggerate, judge others, play a role to impress, or feel insecure around a particular person; this is all good stuff.

I am not unaware of the millions of people each day who consider suicide, or are taking anti- depression medication, or the ones that die and suffer of starvation, neglect, and abuse. Nor am I ignorant of the wars, killing and injustices committed every single day in the name of religion, politics and peace. But I see more deeply the role of each of us in taking responsibility for our own lives, pausing, looking deeply and acting out our sense of responsibility.

On retreat in Plum Village, France, I spent many months with a cotton bearded Vietnam War veteran who inspired honesty, he was a delight to be around and often we would talk late into the night. He spoke about his difficulty being at Plum Village, a practice centre in the Vietnamese Zen tradition. The many Vietnamese children, nuns and monks reminded him too closely of those he had seen during the war and he suffered so much. I have never forgotten the answer given to him by the teacher that day, Venerable Thich Nhat Hanh. My friend was asked to forgive himself and to live very deeply in the opportunity that the new day presented. He may have been their enemy in the past, but today he can offer them his hand in peace. I mention this story because although, I may not be starving, or trapped in a war, wealth has not saved me from what Mother Teresa called 'spiritual deprivation', as so-called first world westerners, we are quite rich, but we still struggle to be truly happy; a growing majority still feel isolated and they still paint their faces each day and live a life that seems disconnected and barely tolerable.

Completely reliant on external conditions our happiness becomes something random and although we make priority out of our mortgages, marriages and retirement, we never ask what are wisdom, spirituality and happiness.

Spirituality begins with the simple knowledge that we as human beings suffer, we experience stress, worry, anxiety, boredom, anger and jealousy, and all of it takes its toll. By now it should be rather self-evident, as human beings we seem to be accustomed to an inherent 'un-satisfactoriness'. We can distract, suppress, and blatantly avoid ourselves, and many great corporations have used these emotional deficits to their advantage. But ultimately this experience

86

comes back to haunt us, we become restless and sooner or later we are strained to recognise our actual situation in life.

There comes a time when we realise that to suffer is not enough, we have to do something to transform it. It is true we can run away our whole lives, when it gets hot we can turn on the air – conditioner, when we are lonely we can go to the refrigerator, when we are bored we can turn on the T.V, when we feel isolated we can go to the club, but this never fills the hole inside us, it only covers it over with soggy paper.

You see, it is not a frail person that sees the ills of modern society and decides to create a new world. It is not a dull person who decides to pause and wonder what really matters in life. It is not a fearful person who decides to begin climbing often alone and later invites others to come and see what he has discovered. It takes discipline, determination, energy and strength of character. In ancient spiritual traditions this person was aptly named a 'Bodhisattva' what would today be known as a spiritual warrior and for anyone who has honestly attempted to transform and heal, the pitfalls are many and the pats on the back are very few.

The first time I was able to stop running, I felt intense craving and I sat down in a room and didn't move for hours – I cried. It was not a transient experience like the ones underhandedly given to us by alcohol or drugs, it is like the first time you see real suffering, in the face of a child, in the hungry looks of adults, in the pain of neglect, abuse and violence – you will simply never be the same again.

You witness something bigger than your self – centred worries and you think you will never be the same again, but in time somehow the memory fades and your old habits re-establish themselves, if you are brave enough not to look away, you soften.

Empathy is born in your heart, then compassion, and for a period your circle of responsibility opens and although the world becomes heavier for a moment, you become lighter forever. Over the years these experiences have become more subtle, but each one has become a deep part of me, they have taught me many things but these are the most important.

Life comes with very few guarantees, it is unpredictable, it is short, it is like a rushing river and if you fail to act wisely in every moment, you lose it. You lose it because you did not even know you had it. Like a wonderful gift left untouched, you simply did not look deeply enough and notice the miracle of life.

Are we constantly being over-run by unnecessary thinking? Regretting the past and furiously constructing new futures? Are we living as though we will die, as though this body and other bodies are subject to sickness?

These questions allow us to let go, soften and cherish the real wonders of life. We let go of petty disagreements, irrelevant worries, and minor attachments and in the process we become lighter and more real. We learn to stop and see more deeply the real wonders of life. An autumn leaf, clouds, an apology, a sunset shared with friends, an open, honest conversation, a hug, a smile, the blue sky, freedom, forgiveness, peace, happiness, real joyful laughter, a courageous life lived with honesty and gratitude. Each day is a wonderful opportunity to live well, to nourish a healthy mind, to be generous, to connect and to discover the present moment, but it is up to us.

Life is relationship. The relationship we have with ourselves, our friends, our family, the environment, with the world. We are not separate, nor can we ever be separate. The ancient scriptures decree 'One in all, all in one', and if we look deeply we can see what they mean, our parents are in us, our ancestors, our brothers and sisters. If we look much deeper we can see how the tree breathes for us and how the universe is contained within each of our cells. If we do not treat ourselves well, we are disrespecting not only ourselves, but our friends, parents and ultimately the whole world.

By the way we eat, work, and celebrate, we can show our respect for our fellow human beings, for the earth and for the animals, because we are not separate from them. This is very real and if we learn to stop and look deeply we can see this and we will be transformed. The way we speak and listen can inspire joy and confidence that can transform the lives of so many. The programs we watch, the internet sites we view, the books we read all water seeds deep in our minds that allow us to experience greater freedom or more of the same old suffering.

We must encourage friendships and communities that bring to life our deepest aspirations for happiness, peace and love. For love comes from relationship, it comes from the depth of our honesty, if our relationships are superficial so is our life. It is from this understanding that we realise food, shelter and transport are significant, but only so we can share them with and fill them with love and meaningful relationships.

The most wonderful mantra that I have ever been offered is 'My darling I am here for you'. If we give the gift of this mantra - our real presence, if we are present for our darling, then she will bloom like a flower. If we stop at the end of each day and ask ourselves have I loved well? Have I been true and honest? Have I used this wonderful gift wisely? And if we answer 'yes' I am positive you will never have any regrets.

Life must be lived in the present moment, for if we live this moment well, all the rest will take care of itself. If we walk deliberately, speak what is true and helpful and courageously confront our own ignorance in every moment, we will be granted the title Bodhisattva. This is not easy, for in the end we must be happy to do our best without too many expectations, we must work diligently for peace within ourselves and not worry too much if others do not understand our efforts. We must walk the spiritual path as a modern day Bodhisattva, doing what we think is right, without too much thought of ever receiving anything in return. We do it for others, for the world and of course we do it for ourselves. Society will try to pull us back in line, our habits will also, but we must courageously walk each day, with a soft purposeful step and unhurried gaze. For the good we do may never be repaid to us, but it will never go unnoticed.

The spiritual path is not about wearing a robe, or heading off to church on Sunday, it is not about being a vegetarian, abstaining from sex and alcohol or having few possessions. These are only forms that we become fascinated with. The heart of the path is about becoming lighter, happier, more peaceful and living deeply in the present moment as it is, not as we would wish it to be. This is where the war ends, inside each mindful step, with each devoted breath and with each deliberate smile, it is an experiential transformation that enables you to see your ignorance, jealousy, fear, anger, confusion and isolation and transform each of them into wonderfully scented flowers that nourish and sustain you.

The path you walk will depend on many conditions and you will have to be creative and clear about choosing them. There are many paths, but you can only choose one and once you commit don't forget to enjoy the breeze and the smell of each season. But ultimately it's your diligence and wise practice that brings you the moments that help you discover your happiness and wellbeing, the moments that show clearly that you are on the right track.

Somehow it is our difficulties that often teach us the most, and that is why

each day when we wake up, we make another aspiration and begin again

and again for the rest of our lives. After all, spirituality is simply about

being yourself and living the life you were meant to live;

only you know what that means.

Ryokan's Lesson

The Japanese have an age old saying, 'If a nail sticks up, bang it down!' and each time I hear this I wince, surely our culture of so-called individuals can do better than forced obedience. And that is what this is all about. To be 'enlightened' means to see things clearly, to perceive each moment as it is, without adding anything. 'Anarchy' means simply to be a revolutionary in our actions, this is planets away from 'forced' and galaxies away from 'obedience'.

If we look backward in time, we see that change does not happen from the government, the industrial, the political level; it comes from the level of individuals. Passionate, courageous, compassionate individuals who love and care about themselves and others, individuals who simply do what they see is necessary and often this can be very simple and fun. They do it with a joy and lightness that is polar opposite to the reactive, burdened movements of a human being forced to live in the heavy shackles obedient to another man's rules.

Our planet has witnessed many great enlightened anarchist's, India had Gandhi, South Africa had Mandela, America had Martin Luther King, Vietnam has Thich Naht Hahn, the oceans have Captain Paul Watson of the Sea Shepherd, throw in poets, musicians and 'simple fools' like Ryokan and everyone can offer this moment something enlightened. These guys, amongst the billions that have lived this brief dream, have given millions a reason, and a rhythm.

You may agree with Bob Dylan and say 'the times are a changing' there are no more battles to fight; there is no need for an enlightened anarchist. Mandela, Gandhi, they are old hat, out of date, hilter kilter; don't burden us with

92

more things to do! But I'm not, I just want to make things fun again!

You may be right and I may be wrong. But enlightened anarchy is nothing more than opening your eyes and seeing, is there anything difficult about that? It is nothing more than living life fully and having a hell of a lot of fun along the way.

For majority of us the answer is no, most people reading this are extremely fortunate, firstly you have eyes, you can read, the list can go further, but let's just say you are lucky. It would be a shame to waste this precious good luck! So if indeed you want to join our gang of merry enlightened anarchists, we only have one thing left to do. Open up our eyes and look around at all the amazing things that surround us and ask hmm, what should 'I' do?

I will finish with a poem, by a Japanese Hermit monk named Ryokan, he had a heart that was light and often I'm sure to the locals he appeared foolish, but he was very enlightened and most importantly he was very happy.

ALWAYS, when I was a boy,

I would play here and there.

I used to put on my favourite vest

And ride a chestnut horse with a white nose.

Today I spent the morning in town

And the evening drinking amid the peach blossoms by the river.

Returning home, I have lost my way. Where am I?

Laughing, I find myself next to the brothel. Ryokan
(One robe, One bowl)

So this month may we stop and ask ourselves 'where am I?'
'What am I doing?' 'Do I really want to do this?'

93

Change comes from within Friendship

Many of us have the habit of wanting to complete things quickly, of 'multi-tasking', and being carried away by the thinking process and never really enjoying whatever we are doing. In short, we trade thinking about life, for actually experiencing living it.

Recently in Israel, walking along a hot desert highway alone, my mind ran unnecessarily, my worries were palpable and fear rushed through my veins. I 'thought' I could not face this question openly, because I knew the answers would bring up fear.

"I know I am in Israel, walking beside the Negev desert, where the Jews were lost for 40 years! I have been walking for many hours on my way to find a camp nestled in some trees about 6km west of here, I have no water or food and the sun is beginning to burn my skin. My shoulders are sore and my bag seems to be getting heavier. Some young Bedouin kids with their broken brown teeth are following me, asking for food and money, they are picking up rocks and launching them beside me as I walk. Soon the rest of the nomads will arrive and the newspaper will read "Stupid Australian found Dead in Desert". I pretended that I was not scared; after all, I had a beard and friends in high places. None of this thinking helped; in fact it only made me more tired and anxious.

In a way we are all travellers moving along with the stream of life, either choosing or allowing life to choose for us. And maybe if we 'stopped' for long enough we would sense the fear, the anxiety, the craving and the confusion that seems inherent in life. Maybe we would sense something else, but what? And how would we deal with whatever was revealed?

94

Whilst watching a television program during the week which encouraged an audience of 'climate change skeptics' to ask questions to a climate change expert from the university of Melbourne, I was fascinated with how much aggression, arrogance, and closed mindedness this man was met with. I could see these people going through physical pain and obviously experiencing emotional suffering in an attempt to hold onto their truth in the face of another truth.

They did not use this opportunity to explore this wonderful topic 'together', to engage in a 'dialogue', instead they stood apart arms crossed and estranged – by concepts, ideals, and language and like little children they held on tight and hoped they would not be moved. On many levels these people are us.

Who has ever changed their mind? Thought they were right and later found out they were wrong? Held onto ideas and concepts, as if they were solid, unchangeable and real?

Spread news or uttered words they were uncertain of, criticised or condemned others, whether openly or mentally, turned mere speculation into so-called fact and were too hard-headed to smile and ask "Am I Sure?" before we went ahead and created more ripples in the pond of life.

Who has ever 'really' listened, with their whole body and mind, without thinking of a 'smart' answer, without thinking, just listening, with the only intention being to understand?

Whether you are a climate change skeptic or a tree-hugger? A meat-eater or a vegan. Do you believe in God or Science? Catholic God or Hindu Gods? Private or government education? What about yoga or Pilates? Julia Gillard or Paul Hogan? White bread or brown bread? Rastafarian or Hare Krishna? Fork or spoon, marriage, maybe gay marriage, sex before marriage, sex after, sex in between?

Just like a child who will not let go of his favourite toy or a man climbing a ladder, if we do not let go of what we are holding – how can we climb higher, or move forward as friends?

Whilst on retreat in France the Zen Monk Thich Nhat Hanh, affectionately called 'Thay' which means teacher by his students said – "The most important thing (in life) is friendship, Mao Zedong said it was independence, but I say it is friendship. If we have friendship, we already have independence…" He asked to nourish our friendship by stopping with our best friend, our loved ones, our Brothers and Sisters, Mothers and Fathers and asking "Who are you, my darling?" If we think we know them, our love will surely die. In the car, the train, the bus, wherever, "I know you are here, and this makes me very happy – who are you, my darling?" Maybe you will discover many things you did not know before, her real loves and aspirations, her talents, her happiness, her suffering, if you do not do this, how can you say you love her, how can you say you are friends. How can you say you have given friendship a real chance to be?

The real question is 'not' do I have many friends? It is 'am I a good friend?'

"Have you ever stopped and listened, without (mentally) evangelizing, judging or discriminating?"

"Have you even heard the birds, the wind, the bees, and the rain without painting them as good or bad?"

96

"Are you allowing your ideas of how you think things should be, to obscure the ways things actually are?"

"Is your idea of happiness preventing you from being happy?"

"Are you sure?"

Enlightened Anarchy does not begin with a protest banner, a loud speaker and a Molotov cocktail; it is not fuelled by anger, or intolerance, or even by the will to change the world (or anything for that matter). It begins with the recognition that life is wonderfully intricate and complicatedly simple – it is how it is, paradoxes and all. Before you 'think' you 'know' it, it is gone. And if you ever 'think' you know another; you are wrong, look deeper.

The practice of friendship should not be limited to those you know. The Dalai Lama was once asked "How can we give up our prejudice, discrimination and our judgments toward each other (Black/White, Muslim/Catholic, Punk/Hippie, Western/Eastern, Rich/Poor) and be free to live in peace?" The Dalai Lama, as he often does began with a smile of recognition before he said "Maybe if Aliens landed! We would see that we all belong to humanity, to this planet and we would finally join together".

"Am I sure? "And "Who are you, my darling?"

These simple practices are the direct steps toward friendship, with those who are already our friends and those who will now be given the chance. If aliens are to ever consider coming, we will have to clean up this mess we have created and our perpetuating and I believe it begins on the train, in our work places and in our homes, I believe it begins with how we treat ourselves, and our relationship to the world, the oceans, animals, plants, and minerals, I believe it begins with friendship.

A monk walks into a pizzeria. He is overwhelmed by all the choices and mindfully scans the menu board. After many moments of deliberation he chooses and waits patiently for his pizza to be prepared. When it is ready the nice Italian man places it on the bench and the monk passes him a twenty dollar note and it is placed in the till. Waiting and waiting the Italian man smiles at the monk and the monk smiles back. Many moments pass before the monk speaks, "will there be any change?"

"Change comes from within" The Italian man replies.

The Easy Way Out

"Everyday forty thousand children die in the world for lack of food. We who overeat in the West, who are feeding grains to animals to make meat, are eating the flesh of these children" Thich Nhat Hanh

With each of your actions, no matter how small and disconnected they may seem, you are supporting and standing up for something. What type of person you are, is easily assessed by how you interact with the world. Next time you put something on to wear or something in your mouth reflect on the source, the chain of events that brought it to you and see how you feel.

Next time you eat a hamburger or a steak – take a moment to reflect.

Evan Sutter

Did you know that a single hamburger patty uses enough fossil fuel to drive a small car twenty miles and enough water for seventeen showers (remember huge parts of the world still don't have clean drinking water!), or that it costs us fifty five square feet of tropical rainforest to raise and produce one quarter pounder burger, or that the worlds cattle alone consume a quantity of food equal to the caloric needs of 8.7 billion people. More than the earth's entire population!

When you eat meat you are saying that it is OK to view animals as machines that pump out milk, eggs, hotdogs, steaks, pork chops, breasts and thighs etc. etc... When you nonchalantly purchase chicken you are saying that it is OK for animals to have miserable lives, living in their own excrement, express grown on growth chemicals to the point that their legs cannot hold them up, with their beaks literally snapped off (often without anesthetic, many dying from shock!), so in the madness of the cramped conditions they do not continue to peck each other to death. This is only one example.

And you are happy to put this in your body, your children's bodies? If you knew how badly animals are treated, in factory farms, if you knew how severe and cruel the production of so-called 'cheap' meat products is and how many repercussions it has, how would you choose to act then?

"The greatness of a nation and its moral progress can be judged by the way its animals are treated" Mahatma Gandhi

When you purchase your 'expensive' beauty products, your fancy shoes and jackets – the only statement you make to someone who is not in a 'cultural trance' is – it is OK to
99

imprison, torture and mistreat other beings, you can rationalize your wrinkle free skin, but when it is built on the back of such ugliness and suffering, how can you say you are beautiful?

We look at the Japanese whaling vessels, the shark fin industry and the killing of black and endangered dolphins and scorn these killings as barbaric. But we continue to support our own cultural cruelties! – The large indiscriminate scrape and haul tactics of factory fisheries that kill turtles, whales, dolphins, sharks, seals, and birds and in turn sell what they don't need as 'by- catch' to farmers to plump up cattle! When we buy our shiny salmon, our omega 3's, our brain food; you support so much more than healthy brain function!

"The question 'Is this right or wrong?' becomes 'Is this going to work for me now?' Individuals must answer it in light of their own wants."
Peter Singer.

This is not about becoming a 'vegetarian' or a 'vegan' (Even if it is clear that eating a plant based diet causes the least amount of harm to yourself, the planet and all creatures!). It is not about purchasing 'ethically', for many; these are only words, symbols. It is about standing up for something beyond your little self, beyond 'I' 'Me' and 'Mine' and seeing that for compassion to really be compassionate- it cannot and does not discriminate! When we choose to 'over-eat', day-in and day-out, these actions have an impact on the world, when we choose to eat meat, fish, dairy, I believe we are over-eating, we are taking advantage and we are eating the flesh of the millions who go without.

100

You do not have to travel to third world countries to make a difference (Air travel presents another diabolical environmental/ethical dilemma!); your everyday actions can change the world! Next time you purchase a product, ask yourself "what am I supporting, what am I standing up for? What kind of world do I want to live in? My children to live in?

In 1944, a fifteen year old named Anne Frank, while hiding from the Nazi's wrote in her famous diaries, "We have many reasons to hope for great happiness, but… we have to earn it. And that's something you can't achieve by taking the easy way out."

FURTHER READING

FOR A FUTURE TO BE POSSIBLE: Buddhist Ethics for Everyday Life –
Thich Nhat Hanh

HOW ARE WE TO LIVE?: Ethics in an Age of Self-Interest –
Peter Singer

JIVAMUKTI YOGA: Practices for Liberating Body and Soul –
Sharon Gannon and David Life

THE DIARIES OF ANNE FRANK –
Anne Frank

Peace

Diary Entry 2nd Jan '10'

9am Ha hagana Train Station Tel-Aviv Israel

It does not make me feel protected to see young men and women dressed in heavy army gear carrying what look like small automatic assault rifles. On the contrary, I am somewhat concerned for them, for this small country and for the world.

They also carry energy drinks, cigarettes and tired, sad faces. Maybe I am too uninformed, too unaware of the whole situation to judge, but I see them and they see me and we smile, but I do not feel at peace. Moments later I am asked for my passport, for the third time in this very short day, I do not feel safe. Who put them in this position? Was it me? Was it the same demons that exist within each of us? Anger, pride, ignorance, hatred, sorrow, restlessness – are these the enemies they are preparing to put holes in?

I wondered. Have we been attempting to fix the out-side world without fixing that which perceives, knows and attempts to understand it? Have we wasted our time and created a heartless monster? Maybe if we could put down our weapons and our differences, we would see something else – but what?

Maybe a year off for the whole world, or at least until we are well again. Think of it as sick leave. To look within will be very difficult in the beginning, but our intention for peace within must be the precursor for our attempt at peace on the outside.

Today I will begin for us all.

102

Evan Sutter

Diary Entry 19th March '10'

1030am Plum Village France – talk by long-term resident and wise gentleman.

"I do not want to have sex" "I do not want to walk" "I do not want to breathe" "I do not want to smile" "I do not want to do cooking" "I do not want to see anymore sunsets" "I do not want to be happy" "I do not want to sweep" "I do not want to eat" "I do not want to meet people"

"I just want to be mindful".

Diary Entry 6th May '10'

430am Mangrove Mountain New South Wales – Satyananda Yoga Academy

Last night I was amazed at how instinctively, I was sorting out who I liked and didn't like, I had a comment for each of them. As I ate in silence, I was rapidly judging them all based on absolutely nothing besides how they looked. A succession of meditation retreats and still this mind only slowly reveals how restless I am, it is constantly smacking me in the face with the murmuring, scheming, comforting, perversions of the everyday-mind.

"I want that!" "How can I get that" "Oh, I don't like that" "more, less" "she did not do that!" "He hurt me!" this infantile interior life was revealed to me over and over and I could see no place for peace amongst the obsessive seeking out of pleasure and avoiding of pain. Was anyone else experiencing this? Am I the only one who is relentlessly thinking?

Diary Entry 10th Dec '10'

555pm Sydney New South Wales Australia

I don't have so many important questions. Today there is only the sound of rain and a candle flickering on the table near where I sit. I used to believe life was not worth living, because I could not find its meaning. Now I think the opposite. It is surely a miracle. When the way I sit, walk and talk affects the happiness of those around me, I see there is nothing else to do, we must act… and so every day I wake up and do my best, after all it is the least I can do. I am grateful and I try to walk for myself and for those who cannot.

This year I found a little peace. It is for the young people I met in Israel, it is for you. It is for all of us.

The Somnambulist

For the past week I have not been able to sleep. I am exhausted. Each night I roll from side to side trying to relax enough to pass the threshold, it comes, but soon I awake again wondering why it still isn't morning. The sun eventually arrives with the vain hope that tonight will be different, and the day is spent sleep walking. I can't sleep and I can't wake up. I feel trapped in the seventh
104

dimension…

Yesterday I forgot my mobile phone number, what I had for lunch and for a moment I did not know how old I was… in a way it was fantastic!

The next day as I watched my Grandfather sleeping I wondered, "What if I forgot everything?" – would I be like a child, like an animal, would I be free to sleep? And in a way I came to envy animals, they live and they die, but they do not seem to make a problem of it, their lives have few complications, unlike ours. They eat when they are hungry or when they are fed, sleep when they are tired and anxiety doesn't seem to play a role in their lives, as far as I can see they are so busy doing what is presented at the moment, that they do not care much for judging or finding meanings out in the future.

For an animal the moment is enough, but humans are much more concerned with avoiding, entertaining (mostly ideas) and prolonging, often our expectations get in the way. We can put up with an extremely miserable present, if our expected future is as we planned. Here is a person who has to go back to work after the weekend, she is surrounded by friends and good times, she has good food to enjoy and yet her power to relish these things is diminished, she is insensitive to the conditions of happiness that surround her; she is preoccupied with something that is not yet here, she ruins the present moment and is helpless to do anything about it. Why?

For her the future is more a reality than the present. She is a special kind of somnambulist, lost in past anxieties and future fantasies, with little idea how to enjoy the present.

Wake Up!

The bells sounds, the children play, the wind touches your skin...

Stop, Listen, Look...

This is a deep part of genuine happiness, it has everything to do with the cultivation of our capacity to pay attention, to be present for the seemingly trivial moments that provide our lives with so much meaning and joy, it has everything to do with healing our society's attention deficit disorder, and it has everything to do with sleeping well at night and waking up fresh in the morning.

What makes you happy?

Addicted to Consuming

Yesterday I was invited shopping, for an item that needed 'upgrading'... I declined and wrote this instead. Did you know that "if parents fail to meet their child's need for soft and firm love, boundaries, respect, trust, time to share and encouragement... they substitute these needs for materialistic wants, but as this fails to satisfy the aching need within, the child craves more and more..." and ends up buying 'stuff' every chance she gets. Dr. J Irvine

Enlightened Anarchists express your social activism by saying no to blatant consumerism; say enough to exploitive mega corps and the ugly face of corporate capitalism by not buying things to satisfy your craving, by avoiding
106

shopping malls, catalogues, internet shopping and fast foods and by expressing your curiosity by looking into our present situation. Our preoccupation with entertaining, consuming and youthfulness and our government's preoccupation with profit, deflect us from taking effective action on such issues as the greenhouse effect, acid rain, salmon depletion, forest destruction, and water contamination.

Only the perversion of global economics would destroy the very air, water, soil and biodiversity that in actual fact are our life support systems, why do we think we are so smart and our technological advancements are so worthwhile, when they are absolutely nothing if the system (we cannot even understand) that supports us, is destroyed in the process.

"Global economics… is a complete perversion" (Suzuki, D.2003) It is a chauvinistic invention, a human creation based on the idea that humans can exploit anything that is of value to 'our' species. As long as humans can garner profit from it, it has worth. In the process huge corporations sell overpriced disposable goods to needy western consumers (who really need another pair of shoes!), while much of the Third World is seduced into mortgaging their futures by the selling of irreplaceable capital in the form of natural resources, while they work like slaves so westerners can have their fix.

Why do 20% of the world's populations consume 80% of its resources?

Why does the world spend 12 times more on military expenditures than on aid, energy, health or education?

Why do 13 million hectares of forest disappear every year?

107

Why are species dying out at a rhythm 1,000 times faster than the natural rate?

If you are awake enough to call yourself an Enlightened Anarchist you must look deeply and instigate some action – we can do change to the world in simple ways…

Enlightened Anarchy is calling for 'Wise Consumption' and this is how it is done:

Live simply, don't buy stuff you don't need

Be curious and think of other people, species and rivers

Find meaning in your life, don't let big corporations define you as a 'consumer'

Get in touch with your emotions, especially craving, and restlessness. If these feelings are present just stop and relax, whatever you do don't fill this place with toys.

Press mute when advertisements come on the television, or better yet, don't watch it! Take a week off and see how this effects your mental state

Get in touch with life, be with friends or make new ones, go for a walk, learn the name of bird, a tree and encourage young people to live life free from fancy labels.

Evan Sutter

You are the World

"To destroy the balance outside of us is essentially, to damage the balance inside of us, for the line between me and you and us and the world is erroneous"

When the Buddha said "the self is made of non-self-elements" he became one of the earliest environmentalists and humanitarians, he saw very clearly that the nature of being human is the nature of what Thich Nhat Hahn calls the nature of inter-being. To be is to inter-be, for obviously we cannot be alone. The human being is a complex of many substances such as oxygen, water, magnesium, calcium, iron, clouds, earth and sun... in essence the human being is made of these and many other non-human elements. We know that our body is over 70% water. How can this water be separate from the water that falls from the clouds?

To destroy the balance outside of us is essentially, to damage the balance inside of us, for the line between me and you and us and the world is erroneous. It does not exist and because we are ignorant of this fact, we kill ourselves slowly. We throw our garbage away and somehow it ends up inside us.

In an open letter address to a UNESCO delegation Zen Teacher Thich Nhat Hanh wrote;

"Only collective awakening can help us solve the difficult problems in our world like war and global warming... I will propose that UNESCO organize a Global No Car Day – a day when people refrain from

109

using their cars, except in emergencies… UNESCO can promote this day around the world and use it as a means to educate and inspire collective awakening concerning the present environmental dangers facing all of us on planet Earth. I will suggest that UNESCO itself, from the director to the ambassadors and other members, try to live in such a way that the message becomes a true message; not just a call for action, but action itself. In our daily lives, we should each try to drive a car that doesn't pollute the environment, or ride a bicycle more often, or use public transportation. Every one of us can do something to protect and care for our planet. We should live in such a way that makes a future possible."

I don't believe it is possible to change the world by changing public policy, I believe small groups of thoughtful, committed citizens can change the world and throughout history have in fact been the only thing that ever does. We need to look into our own lives, be honest and ask when enough is in fact enough. What can we do without, what can we not do without, what are the real conditions for our happiness. I think you will find they have very little to do with fancy cars, houses, body lotions and breast implants.

What can I do? Is a simple question you may need to ask often? For, every one of us can do something right now, to protect and care for our planet. For protecting our planet is protecting our children's planet and also our children, for every single one of us is made of non-us elements. We are quite literally the world.

Mindfulness is Happiness

In three days it is winter solstice, the time when the suns rotation is lowest and the days subsequently the shortest. It is a nourishing idea to me knowing that winter is in its deepest stage and spring/summer is on its way. I do miss the sunshine to me it's a condition or precursor for so many joyous memories. Although many winter memories are being formed in this very beautiful place. Memories of friendships built on sharing, warming in front of a fire with Vietnamese Monks and Nuns; singing songs in the Bamboo Hall and each morning practicing real yoga, mindfulness yoga, deep yoga.

It is a place of calm and peace mostly because distractions are kept at a minimum. No T.V, no internet, no radio or CD's and no newspapers, quite simply put, you are stuck with yourself. When you become restless there's nowhere to go, when you become lonely you have to share with friends or sit and explore the root of this feeling.

I feel after one month why people become attached to places like this, for their capacity to allow deep peace to eventually surface. Of course you must overcome years of craving for chocolate (food), sex (women), activity (distraction) in short we must learn to stop and relax. When this happens all the talk of 'letting go' and 'living in the now' becomes a minor reality, but it is enough to prove to you that such a place really does exist.

The question for me has always been 'is it possible to create this mental posture and maintain it in a normal family and working environment'?

Not everyone can devote themselves to Monastic life, nor should everyone want to. I believe that happiness and
111

peace can be reality on both sides of the tradition (monk/nun – layman/women) without giving up parenthood, intimacy, sex, motorbikes, the beach and the beauty of travel, family life and the rigour of working. I do believe however that happiness lies deeply in ethical living, in virtue, morals, in a love for all things, in taking good care of our health through exercise, meditation, community interaction and generosity. It lies in choosing peace over money (passion for ethical work) and in being diligent in cultivating compassion, generosity, loving, kindness and peace.

This may seem abstract but here it is put into action under the guise of 'Zen Buddhism' with its many foundations, although held up by this practice called 'mindfulness'.

Sila (morals), Smriti (mindfulness), Prajna (wisdom) simply put when you attempt to do no wrong (harm no one, manipulate, coerce, trick, abuse) or are atleast deeply aware when you do, you attain a sense of mental peace. When you practice cultivating stillness and bring your attention deeply into the present moment no longer in the past nor the future (a lifelong project built in years of meditation whilst walking, sitting, lying down, standing up, when I say meditation I mean, a sense of being present to what is happening right now in the breath, body, feelings and the mind holding onto that 'presence' in all situations) we attain this mental state (mindfulness) and we see how we discriminate (he's ugly, she's from America, he has a degree, must be smart) how we avoid, repress and like and dislike. (I can't do that they'll think I'm stupid, I feel lonely maybe I'll have a drink, I will love that because)

These thoughts move continuously in our minds and often we get so caught up in them that our life becomes one 'habitual reaction'. While our sense of self grows and

112

diminishes depending on the situation and we feel stressed, anxious and overcome by the play of the mind. (My name is Nathan, a teacher, an uncle, a son, john is a professor, he must be smart and he's also very good looking, oh' Nathan doesn't feel very good anymore)

Until my calm, peaceful mind sees how ridiculous this all is and smiles at itself for being so 'lower order' and vows to become 'higher order' – not 'higher order thinking' anymore but 'higher order mindfulness'. When this energy (mindfulness) is present it sees my habits (another energy) and by recognising my unwholesomeness energies and looking deeply into them they begin to change. Simply; I stop allowing unwholesome consumption (rubbish into my mind, regret etc.) by being in a good environment and keeping good company. This allows my mind to rest and in this resting state I see things deeply and clearly and come to the roots instead of hacking at the leaves.

Of course, it is not enough to simply know all of this, it only comes to life through practice, friendship and diligently walking, consciously breathing and sitting until it makes sense.

Karma

"Like gravity, karma is so basic we often don't even notice it"
Sakyong Mipham

As a friend to airy discussion, I often hear people talk heartily about 'karma', "Karma will get you!" the mother said to her daughter. "Leave it to Karma" the lazy man stated or my least favorite "It must be your karma…" I avoid the karma debate and give myself over to confused looks instead. Is this simply another case of bookish skits brutalizing an Eastern word and pretending we get it? Does anyone get it? And if we restore 'Karma' to its rightful place in the word chain can we all live happily ever after?

Karma is a Sanskrit word that simply means 'action'. But it also shares a unique similarity with the etymological meaning of the word 'drama'. Insofar as 'drama' in Greek literally means "action" also. As Frank Jude Boccio points out in his commendable book 'Mindfulness Yoga', that each time we add to, fantasize, judge, or manipulate our basic sensory experience , in essence each time we 'dramatize' our thinking, we are creating our karma. He notes how "Everyone knows a "drama queen" who always seems to be embroiled in complexity and turmoil" but we fail to see that we all do this to some degree every single day.

I was once told a story that described Karma perfectly. As long standing poet and meditation teacher Thich Nhat Hahn has seen many changes in the practice centre he shares in France named Plum Village.

He once told a story about a nun named Sister Jinna. Sister Jinna often made the 5am walk from her sleeping room to
114

the big meditation hall at Lower Hamlet. There was a long stone path that weaved around the persimmon trees, built many years ago when the original hermitage was founded. This was the path she and the other nuns and visitors walked each morning en route to practice sitting meditation.

This was their karma and the karma of the Lower Hamlet, set out many years earlier and ingrained in their habit energies. But just as karma is about 'actions' it is also about action. It is about what we do with what we have and also about how we integrate that into our moment.

Sister Jinna saw one morning that she had a choice. And in that moment she created something beautiful.

She walked off the old path and onto the wet grass; she headed down the hill, between the orange scents of persimmons and happily arrived at the meditation hall. What she did not realize is that one day her path would be etched deeply in the ground and each morning many people, thousands over the years, would have a choice. Many chose her path.

Every moment we have the option to step gently in the direction we wish to travel. We have the option to experience life 'just as it is' without wishing things were different, without adding or subtracting to the bare experiences of life. When we cease feeding, energizing or fighting with ourselves and the world, when we become less reactive and more response-able, we choose our own path in life and allow others a peaceful space, free of the karma drama.

Study

"If you want to get laid, go to college. If you want an education, go to the library." Frank Zappa

Study also known as learning doesn't and shouldn't have a life span. As a human being actively seeking knowledge should always be happening sub – consciously, consciously and ever evolving. A university is a learning centre where the world is a learning epicentre.

Too much focus is put on future careers and thoughts of status and money when young people sit down to decide a path of study; this usually involves deciding on courses, Universities and Tafes and much debate stems down to what will put you in the best place to achieve great success in your future. It sounds simple and most people see it as this simple decision.

How can a young person straight out of school be expected to simply pick a course and enjoy it while they enjoy a significant lack of life experience? Why is sitting down with your careers advisor at school an accepted vehicle for decision making? Too much onus is put on getting accepted to university and courses immediately after school finishes and this pressure forces young children to jump into something largely because of these secondary influences, neglecting their passion and loves along the way.

Everyone seems to be in this great rush, because everyone else is in this great rush too, people view getting accepted to courses as great successes and these 'successes' force people to rush straight into to full time study at
116

universities. But how can an eighteen year old kid know what to commit themselves to for three to four years with a significant lack of experience in life in general?

People need to take their time and not follow others but follow their heart instead. Passion needs to be at the top of the agenda to stop the chronic unhappiness that is all too common in society today. You need to genuinely want to learn something not because of other factors like status, job, money or family pressures.

The path in which you want to head becomes clearer every day you experience, every day you taste a foreign food, meet a new person, see a new place, so embrace getting out there, travel, work some casual, part time, full time jobs, work in different places, different environments, do this before you make long term commitments.

Today heading straight from school and into study and then career seems to be the default pathway, but the new age of technology brings with it new opportunities and options and traditional pathways aren't the be all and end all.

We change so much, especially in those years just out of school that it would be silly and ignorant to think we should know what to do when the pens go down from our last school exam. At the age just out of school it is especially hard to forge your own path, at a time when your social standing, ego and perception in the eyes of peers is at the top of your agenda, it is even more difficult to think outside the circle and do something different to the crowd. So we are often driven down the path of others, of our parents' ideas and friends actions.

From my group of friends, who like me, made decisions to go to study on at university from limited or in fact no
117

experience in their chosen areas to engage in 3 to 4 years of study and $25,000 in tuition fees. From that group of say 10 to 12, I struggle to see maybe 1 or 2 who are still working in the field or in fact still enjoying their work.

The others are either unhappy doing what they've done, and because they have invested so much time and money into their career development they decide to stick it out in the hope of something. Before they knew it, life has happened; they've got fiancées and wives; mortgages, rent, bills and they simply can't afford to make a change.

The others of this group have luckily acted upon their unhappiness and made change, new career paths, studied other things and have found something that suits them now. They are the lucky ones, who due to circumstance had nothing in their way, allowing them to pursue something more satisfying. That is not an easy decision in any way, admitting wasted time and money.

I say be patient, explore, explore new lands, new environments, people and everything life can offer, simultaneously discovering yourself, it is only then that you can make worthy decisions on your life.

I have learnt more outside the classroom and this is the case for most of my friends, University degrees are great for the C.V and maybe a little bit of work preparation but they lack depth and reality. Time at university is probably better for building relationships and future contacts and learning about responsibilities, battling deadlines and finding balance then the actual skills and knowledge it provides upon departure. In saying that, I did however leave university with some great skills in picking up girls and a great knowledge of what makes a good party.

Focus should be placed on the young school student Sam,

who says he wants to do Marketing. Prior to enrolling in a Bachelor of Business and committing to investing his time and money, that he contacts companies that have marketing departments or marketing and advertising agencies and commits to work experience and internships, real work experience, not the kind you do in Year 10, where you don't get an accurate indicator of the role.

This too puts onus on the companies, which can in turn strongly benefit them if they embrace the idea. From there Sam can ascertain exactly what goes on, the type of people you would work with, the variety of the role, the 9 to 5, the deadlines, the traffic or transport to and from, and the money you would start off on.

Immediately Sam has perspective, perspective he doesn't have if he followed his career advisor, enrolled in the 3 year course, then suddenly gets hit with it 3 years later, 22 years old, $25,000 in debt and realises this isn't the white wedding he dreamed of at his 2 days of university per week and 3 nights working behind the bar.

We need to enjoy the school days and university days and not just worry about good grades. These places are where we establish great friendships and create great memories. As you get older the chances you get to hang out with your best mates become rarer especially in an environment with limited worries and plenty of time. So don't spend your lunchtimes in the library, it's no point getting great grades if you don't have the confidence to talk to anyone and no friends to share it with either.

The whole picture of success at school is based on memorising words and regurgitating it on paper, do that well, and then do that well at university and you will be successful.

Scribbles on the Wall: Lessons Along the Way

Because let's face it knowing that Aboriginals made up something about a big rainbow serpent creating mountains and valleys is really going to set your son up well for the future, knowing Captain Cook sailed into Australia in 1770 is vital for any young child isn't it, what about making ceramic bowls, that's important, turning on a Bunsen burner. Because they are all real life situations you encounter in the real world, forget about for example driver education; because two students might go on to become very successful sculptors and fifteen kids will hallucinate there is giant snakes chasing them, but only everyone will drive or be driven at some point.

So let's make a push for some real life preparation happening in our schools, take the kids to the mountains and valleys, build real fires at camping and get hands on.

And let's face it, if you're relying on teachers at School to be the primary educators of your children while you sit back and watch; then you need to take a long hard look at yourself.

School is great for developing confidence, friendships and communication skills, in some people that is, and if we are to be serious about life preparation at school then more focus should be placed on these areas, and what about complete, in depth units in confidence and communication, arguably two of the most important traits any individual can display. We have all met the super intelligent social retard, bulked up on too much irrelevant information and starved of any real life substance.

Education and learning starts and ends at home, School is important for learning an array of information on a large variety of things, great if you want to win 'who wants to be a millionaire' and great for the ego at a party, but the real things that breed happiness and success can only be found

120

in small doses in the playground, instead they are found in friends and family, travel, adventure, loss, love, experience, mistakes; these are some of the things that build great men and women, and sadly they are too few a commodity at school.

We are always taught that getting a pass mark equals a job well done, well in university it certainly is enough for a degree. With this a well-known fact 'p's equal degrees' students put focus not on learning and developing but instead on finding the best ways to do the least possible work and attend the least amount of classes and still pass and still get that degree. This is the reason why I think mature age students have the right way, they are studying at university because they actually really want to and they are seeking their own individual development and improving their knowledge as their number one motivating factor. I'm not saying these are elements entirely not evident in students straight from school but they are certainly not as common.

Study shouldn't be some one- off hit in order to get a job; its main objective should be for individual betterment and development. With so much pressure and push in schools we tend to forget what the reasons should be, but study and learning should be about continually adding a string to your bow, about developing and improving, it should be ever evolving and dynamic; it doesn't discriminate by age or gender or by financial position.

Study isn't locked to formal courses in accredited colleges, it can mean grabbing that guitar and trying to hit a few notes, it could be kicking back and reading that book, it could be picking up a language down at a mates place, watching a doco on Lions in Tanzania. People think that once they get a degree that's it, but that only prepares them for one very specific set of skills, in order to thrive in life and all its complexities we need a broad knowledge base and this means getting out and getting involved in all of life's wonders.

Here are a few books that can get you started, they are all totally different and all offer something very unique.

A Long Way Gone; Memoirs of a Boy Soldier, by Ishmael Beah

This book is mesmerizing, simply because it is such a heartbreakingly honest account of war and violence and later healing. Ishmael Beah knows first-hand what it means to fight on the front lines, he was only twelve. This book will make you cry, laugh and without a doubt you will never be the same again.

Let My People Go Surfing; The Education of a Reluctant Businessman, by Yvon Chouinard

This book is cool for so many reasons. A world-class mountain climber turned reluctant entrepreneur, creates one of the world's most thought-provoking life stories and a thriving business named Patagonia. "...a moving autobiography, the story of a unique business, and a detailed blue print for hope." (Jared Diamond, professor UCLA)

A Million Little Pieces, by James Fry

Enter a tale of drug addiction and one man's unique experience toward recovery. Originally released as a memoir, until investigators found that pivotal elements were somewhat polished or untrue, this semi-autobiographical tale is hard-hitting, thought-provoking and somewhat gruesome. Read it if you dare, but you will never look at addiction the same way.

The 4-Hour Work Week, By Timothy Ferris

The title of this book can be a little deceiving and in a way make it sound like a scam or a fraud. But it is anything but; Timothy Ferris introduces us to an array of new concepts and ideals and squashes the old concept of retirement and saving for the future. He brings light to living for the now and not waiting for when you are old and grey to enjoy. The 4-Hour work week is a blueprint for escaping the rat race.

Learning from the Heart: Lessons on Living, Loving, and Listening, by Daniel Gottlieb

"What does it mean to be human?" A car accident turned acclaimed psychologist Dan Gottlieb into a quadriplegic at age thirty-three, with two children, a wife, and later a divorce, you wouldn't expect his book to be so generously funny and insightful. It is! The winner of the 'Global Love of Lives Medal' this book is an ode to life and humanity. Perfect.

Inspiration & Motivation

"Twenty years from now you will be more disappointed by the things that you didn't do than by the ones you did do. So throw off the bowlines. Sail away from the safe harbor. Catch the trade winds in your sails. Explore. Dream. Discover." Mark Twain

There will be days when you need a little more. There will be days when you just can't get yourself out of bed or can't get yourself moving. You need to surround yourself with great people; people who are going to drive you and motivate you to act. But sometimes these people aren't always around so in that case surround yourself with the work from inspiring people, Branson, Gandhi, Einstein, throw up pictures of cool places on the walls, fill your laptop with great stories of strength and determination; Surround yourself with inspiration.

Here are some things that get me moving and give me a little focus to get back on track.

YVON CHOUINARD

Founder & Owner of Patagonia

This is so much more than a story about how a man built a thriving business that turns over more than $200 million a year, but a story of a man who never lost sight of the bigger picture, who stuck to his values and principles, who showed amazing vision, integrity, responsibility and courage.

124

He was a pioneer in so many ways, who brought doing good and having fun into the heart of his business, a business that is very much a leader, unique and values led.

He brought the passion of his love for the great outdoors, rock climbing, surfing, fishing, kayaking, skiing and travelling directly into business, and never forgot why he got started and never let the greed of capitalism and the chance of big quick cash get in the way of ethics and his immense vision.

From when he first began designing and manufacturing rock climbing equipment in the 1950's, his strong values were evident. Despite pitons (climbing tool that was hammered into the rock) being the mainstay of his business and the main money maker, he found they were disfiguring the rocks, the once pristine mountain faces he loved so much were becoming destroyed. Many a man faced with this dilemma may choose the easy money, not this one; he stopped the production of pitons and instead designed an environmentally friendly alternative and started the push towards clean climbing.

Later, through the success of Patagonia's clothing line, he learnt industrial grown cotton was the most damaging for the environment , he made the switch, at massive financial costs to 100% organically grown cotton. In 1993 they were the first to start making jackets using fibre from recycled polyester soda pop bottles. His environmental initiatives even flowed onto his buildings, most of his stores our old free standing building saved from the wrecking ball, and one building was built using 95% recycled materials.

Through his passion for climbing and travelling the world, he noticed the deterioration of the natural world and the rapid changes taking place, the forests were disappearing, glaciers were melting and wildlife dwindling. He took it
125

upon himself to make a change, giving away 22 million dollars in donations to grass root conversational activists, helping to save old forests from being torn down, mines from being dug, dismantling damaging dams, restoring rivers, creating parks and wilderness.

He was at the forefront of in work child care centres, at a time when it was new and relatively unknown, his passion for his employees led the way for what is a common practice around the world today. He started the 'let my people go surfing flexitime policy' where employees take time off to catch a good swell, go bouldering or greet their kids off the school bus. He was again ahead of his time in changing the face of the office, removing offices and doors and encouraging a fun and happy workplace. It was these things that made Fortune Magazine list Patagonia in the 100 best companies to work for.

He restrained from selling to mass merchants and department stores, as it challenged his principle of making the best quality products, even though it meant missing out on massive monetary benefits and massive profits at a time when his business and the economy was struggling. He refused to write advertising that appealed to vanity and greed, instead using it to promote environmental concerns. And Patagonia was the first business in the United States to print its catalogue on recycled paper.

In 2001, Yvon, cofounded '1% for the planet', an alliance of businesses that contribute at least 1% of their net annual sales to groups on a list of researched and approved environmental organisations.

Yvon is no doubt a 'beautiful mind', a pioneer, a man of many firsts, a brave soul who drew a line in the sand and forced change. Who throughout his life stayed strong to his principles and as a result formed a business that has

126

flourished. He withstood the temptation of big money fast, and instead formed a business that can be around in 100 years, not just a business after short term success and the quick buck.

He is what you call authentic and so is everything that Patagonia stands for, authentic not just a bunch of meaningless letters, but truly authentic right down to the bone. In his pursuit of the highest quality products, he has caused minimal damage to the environment, something that cannot be said for many businesses around the world, he showed that capitalism and ethics can stand together.

And all along the way, he did something he loved, travelling the world, surfing, fishing, and climbing. Bringing change to important issues and making other businesses around the world sit up and take notice.

For more info on Yvon, check out "Let my people go surfing" the education of a reluctant businessman. It's a great read.

KARL BUSHBY

Adventurer

Not many people would know who Karl Bushby is, but it won't take too long to be captivated by his amazing story. Not too long ago I was in fact one of these people, unaware what this former British Paratrooper was doing, unaware of his feats and of his courage, discipline and unmatched will.

Karl has been, and is, attempting to walk around the world with unbroken steps, a journey that has taken him from
127

the Southern tip of South America in Punta Arenas, Chile, through Argentina, Peru, Ecuador, Colombia, across the Darien Gap, throw Panama, Costa Rica, Nicaragua, Honduras, El Salvador, Guatemala, Mexico, United States, Canada, Alaska, across the Bering Straits and into Russia.

Known as the Goliath Expedition, Bushby began his journey in 1 November 1998 and expects to finish it by 2014 arriving in his home town of Hull England, then having walked over 36,000 miles.

When interviewed by the longestwayhome.com we got a better insight into what exactly drives a man to depart on such a crazy, hell scary adventure.

When asked about any travel tips, Bushby responded "It's like the man said 'just do it'. So many people ponder on making a move but don't act upon their dreams and ideas. More often than not it's out of fear; it's a lack of self - confidence. Our addiction to safety and over abundance of caution can stop us from being the best we can be, can stifle the human spirit. Man has to realise he got where he is today because he was willing to take risks and he will have to take risks again."

Bushby talks of the inspiration he drew from the Ranulph Fiennes and Mike Shroud crossing of Antarctica on foot in 1993, he talks of the fire that was lit, and smouldered in the back of his mind for years, unable to be put out, with only one option left, to just do it. It's crazy to think of the adventures Bushby would have encountered on his travels by foot, avoiding being gunned down by Columbian Guerrillas, the snow storms, the freezing temperatures, day after day of no food, cultural barriers in secluded, untouched lands, the loneliness, lack of sleep and the fear of the unknown.

12 years of travel in the great unknown, doing something that no man has done before him is pretty special.

If we can take one thing from Karl Bushby, it's not necessarily the adventure and the walking around the world, it's his advice, to "just do it", to stop thinking and pondering and start acting on your dreams, start acting on your ideas, forget about the safety and caution, look inside and find the confidence and be the best you can be, a little risk could change your life forever.

You can follow Bushby's journey on his website at www.odysseyxxi.com and at twitter.com/OdysseyXXI

For a more detailed look at his journey Bushby wrote a book about his walk entitled Giant Steps.

CJ HOBGOOD

Professional Surfer

CJ Hobgood is a pro surfer who has been at the top of world surfing for over a decade, rubbing shoulders with the legendary Kelly Slater and battling it out with the new brigade of young pros like Owen Wright and Jody Smith. Yes, the man can obviously surf and surf well, to be around for so long, transcending eras in an ever changing sport, but what makes CJ a beautiful mind is a cause he has put his name behind.

In an era of sport where big dollars are thrown at athletes from big companies to wear their gear, their shirts, shorts, sunglasses, shoes and whatever that can add to their bottom line, CJ Hobgood has used his name to raise awareness for a non for profit organisation. CJ surfed on the world tour (the top tour in world surfing) sponsored by TWLOHA; (To Write Love On Her Arms) a non-profit organization offering help for young people struggling with depression, addiction, self-injury and suicide.

In this day and age it is an absolute rarity to see a big name athlete shun the big dollars on offer in order to help push a cause. And push he did indeed, with the awareness raised through CJs quest, TWLOHA won $1 million in the American Giving Awards, $1 million that will go a long way in helping a whole heap of people in the future.

It's pretty special seeing any person using their name and fame to help the lives of others, CJ could have easily picked up a few sponsors and made a quick money grab before retirement, but instead he used his last few years as a way to make change in people's lives & that's very cool.

Hopefully Mr. CJ Hobgood will be a pioneer for more athletes to follow suit.

QUOTES TO GET YOU MOVING

"We don't stop playing because we get old; we get old because we stop playing"

Too many times in society people conform to what is the norm, you should be doing this by a certain age, you should have this and be like this. And along the way they find themselves in a place they never imagined, a place they don't like.

With all this pressure around us, we forget the simple things in life; we evidently forget what it was like to be young, to have no worries, no commitments. Back then our mind was still, always in the present, now for some it is a never ending jig saw puzzle on a merry go round.

So don't think you can't do something because no one else your age is – have fun. Free yourself from the shackles of expectation and judgement and jump headfirst down that slippery slide, backflip into that pool. For one you will feel amazing, it will give you renewed energy, add a few years to your life and your kids and kid's mates will love you.

"They may turn off the electricity. But the moon will still shine in my window"

This is deep, very deep, but also very, very true. This is about positivity and confidence, two of the most important pillars in life. This is about staying true to what you believe in and knowing through the hard times that you will succeed.

131

Yeah, some bad shit happens, yeah you come across some bad people, but it's about knowing you can do what you do and I will do what I do, you won't stray me from my pursuits, bring me down, heckle me, fire me, evict me, kick me, but I'm still here. Turn off the electricity, it don't matter, I've still got more than enough light and power.

"Don't die with the music in you".

This might just be my favourite quote of all time. It's about regrets. It's about making the most of what you have and not waiting too long before it's gone. Everyone has some beautiful music in them, and it will be a damn shame if you go through life and no one gets to hear it.

So if you have a passion for something, if you believe you can do something, then give it a crack, life is short, people think we live forever, I'll do that tomorrow, next year, I'll wait till I do this then I'll do that. Don't let fear hold you back, the fear of failure, because when someone has the bravery to pursue something, regardless of their level of success, that music is loud and clear for all to hear, you might miss a few notes here and there, but the more you get that guitar out, the closer you are to something beautiful.

"Great spirits have often encountered violent opposition from mediocre minds"

There is always going to be someone who says you can't do something. There's always going to be statistics and facts that say that can't be done. You have two choices, succumb to your fears, give in and believe what is said, living your life never knowing what could have been and as a result seeing out your days with a sense of emptiness.

Or you can stick it to the man, forge your own path, skip the pats on the back for the short term and chase the bigger picture. Imagine if Einstein listened to the doubters. Every great person who has achieved something special has encountered this violent opposition, and it's the very reason that they are great, if they gave in, you would never have heard of them and I would be carving this in stone.

"We must all suffer from one of two pains: the pain of discipline or the pain of regret. The difference is discipline weighs ounces while regret weighs tonnes".

The sacrifices you make now will be little compared to the regret that will come later if you don't commit and strive to take advantage of your opportunities. Regret hurts, it really does and it is something you can never get back. Life is short, it is sometimes extremely short, we need to look at the bigger picture and think what will make me and my loved ones happier.

"Do not depend on the hope of results. You may have to face the fact that your work will be apparently worthless and even achieve no result at all, if not perhaps results opposite to what you expect. As you get used to this idea, you start more and more to concentrate not on the results, but on the value, the rightness, the truth of the work itself. You gradually struggle less and less for an idea and more and more for specific people. In the end, it is the reality of personal relationship that saves everything." Thomas Merton

133

"Ask me not where I live or what I like to eat… Ask me what I am living for and what I think is keeping me from living fully that." Thomas Merton

"You are like a candle. Imagine you are sending light out all around you. All your words, thoughts and actions are going in many directions. If you say something kind, your kind words go in many directions, and you yourself go with them. We are… transforming and continuing in a different form at every moment." Thich Nhat Hanh

"Be yourself. Life is precious as it is. All the elements for your happiness are already here. There is no need to run, strive, search or struggle. Just be beautiful, be yourself." Thich Nhat Hanh

"Wherever we are we have the capacity to enjoy the sunshine, the presence of each other and the wonder of our breathing." Thich Nhat Hanh

Confidence & Discipline

"Man often becomes what he believes himself to be. If I keep on saying to myself that I cannot do a certain thing, it is possible that I may end by really becoming incapable of doing it. On the contrary, if I have the belief that I can do it, I shall surely acquire the capacity to do it even if I may not have it at the beginning." Mahatma Gandhi

Results and success don't come easy, in reality, unless you're extremely lucky, you have to work for things, commit yourself and be disciplined as you strive towards what it is you want. My discipline, or lack of it, has possibly let me down more than any other thing. The few regrets I do have, come down to not chasing after things enough, being to nonchalant, waiting for tomorrow, instead of taking control today.

I find myself still wanting some of the same things I wanted 8 years ago, the reason, being ill disciplined with a massive lack of will power, letting my priorities slip away because of the chance to satisfy my short term desires, sex, drugs and ego. I sometimes think if I stuck some things out, where would I be now, despite being happy in the present; the old thoughts can't help but entertain the idea of something better.

"Laziness is the curse of modernity, choose the untrodden path…the challenge, the heavy load, choose courage – for that will make all the difference"

You will never get anywhere worth- while without discipline, at least not in the long term, from my experiences, the ones who have had success, have been the ones who have made sacrifices, sacrificed minor desires all

135

for what was really important. That is discipline. Knowing what you need or want and making the sacrifices and commitments to get it.

Discipline and Confidence go hand in hand with each other; together they form a mighty partnership. You simply can't understand how being low in confidence can hold you back from everything in life. Confidence is one of the most important assets any person can have, especially a young person.

So many young people these days lack confidence dramatically, they don't know how to look someone in the eye and say hello. The age of technology is a key factor in this problem, they sit in front of a computer, video game all day, not communicating with anyone, not socialising, just stuck in their own little world. They are not used to talking with other young kids, or any one older.

The only contact they get is with the people in their own house and their small group of friends at school. They become comfortable and confident in dealing with these people but as soon as they are in an environment with new people, people from various age groups and various cultures they freeze, become shy and have no people skills whatsoever.

From my family and friends I can see a direct relationship with how much time young children spend alone playing video games and how confident they are. I have found the young ones that play sport, or are involved in other social environments, and are around 10 – 15 other people their age (not just the ones they are comfortable with at school etc.) coaches, trainers, teachers (less formal than a school environment) are far more confident and importantly have far better people skills. Confidence is something that starts young and is something that should be intentionally

136

Evan Sutter

nurtured; there is far too limited emphasis on this. Because there is nothing worse than seeing a 13 year old who can't lift his or her head up and simply say hello, let alone hold a conversation.

This continues as you get older and confidence becomes more and more important. Without it you will struggle to get a job, regardless of your achievements academically. I can vouch for this first hand, when discussing candidates from interviews with the CEO at a past job, the one who was clearly a stand out academically, was unanimously rejected for the confident, people person.

Confidence is a mixture of knowing what you want and knowing that you are well equipped to get it, it is being able to communicate with all kinds of people without being intimidated or overawed, it's being able to hold your head high and look people in the eye and it can go as far as being a leader and not a follower.

It is built through experience, life experience, meeting an array of people and a seeing an array of places. There is a big difference being outgoing and extroverted among those close to you and being able to be that with everyone. A confident person stands out in the crowd, it's in the way you walk and it's in the way you talk. It's the middle ground somewhere between shyness and arrogance.

Life is simply too short to let opportunities pass you by because of fear and lack of confidence. Just think how many questions remain unanswered because you were too scared to ask, how many girls you've let walk away, how many of everything. I would encourage confidence and discipline, how do you get it, by putting yourself in life, by saying hello to strangers, joining teams or social clubs, conversing, knowing what you want and believing you can get it, and knocking down all the obstacles in front of you,
137

until you do.

You need to possess the attitude of not worrying what everyone thinks, especially strangers, because they don't know you and probably never will, so don't let them stand in your way for fear of ridicule or judgement.

As Einstein put it "Everyone is a genius, but if you judge a fish on its ability to climb a tree, it will live its whole life believing it is stupid."

Evan Sutter

Lifestyle

"Get busy living or get busy dying." Stephen King

It's all in the word. Lifestyle. Life and style. The key is to make your life; your style.

It's funny how something as simple as moving to a new place can significantly alter ones mood, attitudes and behaviours. For years I stayed in a place that didn't suit my needs, it didn't suit what I wanted to do. But for the sake of a job I stayed; stuck in the city life, the traffic, the crowds and the noise. The hectic pace never suited me at all and for years I was somewhat of a prisoner trapped in routine and it started to take its toll.

You can talk all you want about a place you love and a place you can really see yourself living, but it takes strength to break the shackles and walk. When you live in a place that suits you and a place you love, the positivism it brings transcends through each day. A nice bushwalk, a swim in the ocean, the fresh sea breeze, and the unfamiliar faces rejuvenate and refresh any staleness that previously existed.

I said for years and years I wanted to get to the coast, to enjoy the beaches, surfing, fishing but it wasn't until I was completely honest with myself that I knew I had no other choice but to take the risk of new job, new friends and a new environment. While new places can be potentially harder to find your most desirable job, being able to do what you love in between makes it all worthwhile.

Everyday back in the city life, the sun rose and it set, but I saw very few of them, but now I do, I lived the same
139

distance from the shops, but I drove; now I walk, I watched TV until I would get to bed, now I walk the dog. A lifestyle change, is as it says, a life change, its life, but more your style.

I'm not saying move out of the city and to the coast, what I'm saying is think deeply about what excites you and where you want to be and stop thinking and stop talking and give it a shot. Worst comes to worst, you can always move back and continue on as normal, knowing that you've tried and you are in fact better suited to your environment. So taste the country if that is what you've always desired, maybe test the big city, by doing so your opening yourself up to new attitudes and behaviours that our filled with positivism and potential.

It seems when we are young we have our high expectations, our big dreams, than we get to a point whether it be at our job, or our family life and everything gets pushed to a side. We get to a position where it becomes too complicated to just 'follow your dreams'. It seems that we are programmed to earn, buy, and live in a material world. Our status is judged by what our bank balance shows and Lifestyle simply doesn't fit into the 'real world'.

We get stuck analysing all the things that might happen; all the things we leave behind instead of believing in what we really want, we make it harder on ourselves for no reason. I say dream big, and have the will to have a crack.

Jon Krakauer, the author of 'Into the Wild' illustrated this perfectly when he said "make a radical change in your lifestyle and begin to boldly do things which you may previously never have thought of doing, or been too hesitant to attempt. So many people live within unhappy circumstances and yet will not take the initiative to change

140

their situation because they are conditioned to a life of security, conformity, and conservatism, all of which may appear to give one peace of mind, but in reality nothing is more dangerous to the adventurous spirit within a man than a secure future. The very basic core of a man's living spirit is his passion for adventure. The joy of life comes from our encounters with new experiences, and hence there is no greater joy than to have an endlessly changing horizon, for each day to have a new and different sun."

Too many people are a product of their environment, they let it shape them, it dictates what they do, where they do it, what they wear, what they believe in, instead of being the one who actually shapes their own environment, the one who finds out what is best for them and does accordingly. Environment also plays a telling role in an individual's IQ; that is the people they are surrounded by, the things they do in that environment and so on, this demonstrates how important it is to find your lifestyle, one that suits you, because it has a bigger impact on you every day that you could have ever imagined.

There are so many little subtle differences between one place and another and they become more apparent when you spend some more permanent time there. From my individual experiences and the experiences from my friends and family who have made a big move these subtle differences are the differences that manage to change your perceptions and mindset.

I have made many moves from various places depending on work and the need for something fresh. One such temporary move involved moving back from the coast to where I grew up in the suburbs some 50kms outside from the major city. The changes in culture and lifestyle were drastic and it was here that again I realised the importance
141

of where you live and its direct correlation with happiness and positivity.

A few months earlier you would catch up after work for a surf or quick hit of tennis, maybe a run or box or some sort of exercise. In the mornings you would rise early and grab a coffee and brekky down at one of the many local cafes with a group of mates, there you would catch up with friends, have a chat, laugh and make plans for the week ahead.

During the week we would catch up for dinner at the local pub or a new restaurant or someone would get everyone over their house for dinner. It seemed you were always surrounded by plenty of people, always had plans and plenty of adventures. Looking back they were all just simple things, easy things that anyone can do.

Finding myself back at my hometown this approach to life was unheard of, there was very little midweek contact with mates if any at all, despite the fact I had a bigger bunch of friends there; it seemed people were too busy engulfed in their own lives to make time to catch up for dinner or a coffee.

They chose to watch T.V instead of catch up with mates. Despite my friends in both areas having the same amount of singles and couples and both having jobs and other demands, people in the area on the coast seemed to make socializing and surrounding themselves with friends and family one of their priorities.

It was surprising to see how quickly I fell into this way of living despite how reluctant I was; I went weeks without seeing anyone even though I was closer in proximity to a greater number of friends. My exercise decreased when the solo sessions lost their enjoyment and my social life
142

followed when the only chance for a catch up had to include ten beers; as males can't catch up with each other for a coffee, at least not in this town.

Quickly my passion for life and overall positivity was on the decline because of something as simple as a different lifestyle choice. This was a great lesson as to the amazing effects your place of residence has on your entire life.

I had friends who had recently moved to the area for work and talked about how there was nothing to do, they had a better job with more opportunities but were struggling and not liking the day in day out, because they didn't have all the little simple things that they took for granted or took for just part of life back at home.

We can all take the easier option and idol through our lives with little fuss and forget our dreams; work our butts off in a 'good job' and look forward to retirement. But it's the fuss, the dreams, our lifestyle, every day and every night; it's taking that scary step into the unknown that makes us who we are and keeps us fresh.

Respect & You

"Man did not weave the web of life; he is merely a strand of it. Whatever he does to the web, he does to himself" Chief Seattle

Respect has been a common theme since the beginning of man; it is prevalent in the bible and is something drummed into us since childhood from parents, family, friends and teachers. Many people, especially the older generations argue that respect is a diminishing commodity. They argue that there is a newfound disrespect not only for people but for the land as well. The old saying "treat people, like you would like to be treated" may well be on the endangered list.

Why is respect so important? Because with a total lack of respect for our fellow man. The world would spiral uncontrollably into chaos.

Respect is one of the most important values that I try my hardest to live by, and try my hardest to pass onto my nephews, nieces and younger friends. Respect for ourselves, respect for others and respect for our environment are critically important.

Our society is becoming more and more superficial and materialistic with every new ad campaign that storms into the younger generation's faces, magazine covers are littered with thin, perfect-bronzed models; every ad targets our insecurities and persuades us to believe that without the latest trend we cannot be cool or popular. Instead of creating people of unique substance and style we encourage conformity.

144

This leads to young people disliking themselves as they chase unrealistic targets that they see every day in the media and this creates false perceptions of what they should look like or act like and it is causing challenges for them to overcome in order to truly appreciate themselves as they are, which is paramount in every way for them to love themselves; which is where respect begins.

How are we to respect someone else if we do not respect ourselves, respect who we are, what we believe, in, all that we stand for. Respect begins from within us. To be comfortable with whom we are physically, to accept and embrace all our flaws and weaknesses and to realise we are all individuals is necessary if we are to respect ourselves and in turn respect others and the environment at large.

As a teenager I was quite ignorant when it came to being respectful to others, I found it hard to learn my lessons well, my stubbornness blinded my perceptions, therefore the decisions I made were never in my best interest. I was brought up to respect others, but never seemed to fully grasp the concept. I was taught respect should be earned. It took me a long time to realise we should respect everyone for exactly who they are, regardless of how they dress or look, or how much money they earn, everyone deserves to be given respect, from the young innocent child to the greying old man.

Respect shouldn't be something we have to earn, it should be automatically given. At the risk of sounding a little cliché, if we can strive to see that everyone has something to offer and show true respect to all of mankind without letting race, gender or age hinder our vision; our communities, work places and all of society will benefit.

With the shift from traditional family households many young people are missing out on the respect that is taught

145

in the family home, the discipline from the father, the love and care from the mother. More than ever, the onus is now placed on the individual, and that is exactly how it should be, we all are responsible for our own actions, and we all our responsible for how we treat our fellow man.

Being rude, ignorant and arrogant are sure ways to gain no respect from anyone and being respected by your peers, by strangers, by elders, from within and outside your family is one of the greatest accolades any individual can receive. Being successful in your chosen field but having no respect from the people you work with and the people within the field really takes away from your successes; the person who achieves both is truly successful.

My uncle gave a speech at his son's 21st, that 5 years on I remember vividly. He said that if you can live life and the people around you, your work friends, family, childhood friends, people from the area say something as simple as you are a good man, then you are a success, living with that respect from everyone around you, really is a great privilege.

Can we forgive ourselves for being human; can we love ourselves as we are? Warts and all? Because if we cannot see ourselves clearly and make peace with that love inside us, how can we love someone else? This means looking at those things that bring us happiness, looking at our goals, our aspirations, our relationships and looking at our strengths and weaknesses.

Do not wait to enjoy the joys of life; before you know it they are gone. Say and do what needs to be done to bring joy to yourself and those around you.

Evan Sutter

Strength & Violence

"Nothing is so strong as gentleness, and nothing is so gentle as true strength" Ralph Sockman

Too often today strength is confused for physical strength, how big you are, how fast you run, how heavy weights you can lift. These are great for various occupations and vocations but are quite petty when put in context of the everyday world.

Young people pride themselves on being the biggest, strongest and fastest, they push themselves through exhaustive training regimes to have the biggest biceps and then society slaps them with the label that they are strong and tough. More often than not it's these trivial pursuits and unwarranted pats on the back that create issues for younger generations.

It is all too common today to see young men bulked up on steroids. What once was the domain of elite athletes and sportspeople has flowed into the general public. Steroids aren't being used for illegal and unethical advantage in sport but for purely cosmetic purposes to look good for the beach and music festivals. It is sad to see how shallow parts of society have become that they feel the need to cause endless damage to their bodies so their biceps look attractive to other equally shallow people.

Doing weights and training is done for the purpose of benefiting your health, doing steroids and lifting heavy weights is a direct contradiction to this. Elevated blood pressure, harmful changes in cholesterol levels, liver damage, reduced sexual function and temporary infertility,
147

major issues with the heart including cardiac arrhythmias, congestive heart failure, heart attacks, and sudden cardiac death. Then there's the aggression and violence, mania and less frequently psychosis and suicide associated with steroid abuse.

Is it really worth it?

You can't grow up thinking these are great attributes to attain and chase because they only satisfy very shallow short term needs. We shouldn't confuse this type of strength with 'real' strength and we must educate our young ones that it takes a whole lot more than a bench press to determine ones strength.

These false associations of strength with force and power are very dangerous associations especially with young people desperately trying to fit in with everyone around them. We should encourage the cultivation of discipline, love, kindness and our own individual personalities and substance.

Strength is not beating up someone for petty kicks and the applause of friends, strength doesn't exist where there is fear. But because this association of strength with power and force is so heavily entrenched in our biological makeup it is difficult for people young and old to identify with real strength and it results in so much fighting and violence that is present in our society today.

I wonder how much fighting and unnecessary assaults would be avoided if this false association was unmasked? How many nightclub glassing's would be prevented if our need to satisfy our ego and the approval from friends wasn't such a high priority? If we didn't think that knocking someone out made us tougher and stronger?

Is it not the stronger man who walks away from a fight, despite the jeers from friends and the effects on their reputation? Is the stronger man the one who can turn down the offer of drugs and alcohol again despite the peer pressures and insults? Is the stronger man the one who helps the old lady up the stairs despite no recognition from anyone? Or is it the person willing to help a mate when he is in need and doesn't ask?

Strength is honesty and integrity and comes from the heart, it is not physical. It is giving respect and kind words even when they are difficult to give. It is being respected not out of fear but out of love. This is the strength that young people should strive for because this other thing that is far too commonly referred to as strength is short term and only temporary, whilst this kind of strength, this 'real' strength can last a life time.

Mahatma Gandhi said "The weak can never forgive. Forgiveness is the attribute of the strong" and "Strength does not come from physical capacity. It comes from an indomitable will." these are the kind of attributes and associations of strength that we should be focusing on, not speed, nor power.

We mistake physical strength for real strength all the time and I saw this valuable life lesson firsthand in a friend named Scott. Scott was a big brute of man known for his size and more so for the fact that he was the best fighter in town. It was a weekly occurrence that Scott would find himself at the pub and in a fight and it was a regular occurrence that Scott would come out on top.

For his efforts Scott was seen as somewhat of a local legend, a well- respected guy with a big reputation. For all at the time Scott displayed qualities that everyone else would seek, his so called strength had made him very

149

popular and feared. These associations sat very well with Scott and it was like he continued to act in such a manner for these labels that where attached. Scott would let his anger and ego and all these associations that had been imprinted into him since birth take control. Scott would pick fights with nice guys minding their own business; he would prey on the weak and humiliate others for simple pleasures.

But it didn't take too long for people to start to ignore and dislike Scott and all his actions that made him popular had actually made him unsociable and difficult to be around. He soon found himself with no friends and a lot of issues.

Scott was perceived to be strong, his name was associated with great strength when in actual fact it was the opposite and Scott suffered great weakness. He let anger and emotions get the better of him to a state where he had no control, he let pressures from people around him influence how he acted and he let ego and social status dictate terms. What he displayed was not great strength but great weakness; there was no indomitable will or forgiveness, no honesty or gentleness.

Scott wasn't strong enough to dismiss the praise from others but instead let it feed his need for status and ego and painfully learnt the hard way that physical force, fighting and violence doesn't make a man or women strong, it actually makes them weak.

Learn from the lesson of Scott and find your own inner strength from below the roots of anger, ego, status and emotion but instead let your strength flow from your heart.

150

Fear

"There are two basic motivating forces: fear and love. When we are afraid, we pull back from life. When we are in love, we open to all that life has to offer with passion, excitement, and acceptance. We need to learn to love ourselves first, in all our glory and our imperfections. If we cannot love ourselves, we cannot fully open to our ability to love others or our potential to create. Evolution and all hopes for a better world rest in the fearlessness and open-hearted vision of people who embrace life." John Lennon

We simply cannot afford to let fear determine the choices we make or don't make in life. Fear is the reason for so many people failing to reach their goals and their dreams. It is responsible for holding back more people from achieving then arguably anything else. The fear of what other people may think, the fear of failure, the fear of financial loss or physical strain, the fear of social condemnation all hold us back from getting to where we really and truly want to be.

As adventurer Karl Bushby said "just do it, So many people ponder on making a move but don't act upon their dreams and ideas. More often than not it's out of fear; it's a lack of self -confidence. Our addiction to safety and over abundance of caution can stop us from being the best we can be, can stifle the human spirit. Man has to realise he got where he is today because he was willing to take risks and he will have to take risks again."

Fear can paralyze you and it can control you, it can stop you from living the life that you dream. We need to sit back from our feelings when we are scared and see what it is exactly which we fear, we need to ask ourselves why am
151

I feeling this way and what can I do to minimize this feeling or destroy it all together.

When we see the real reason why we fear something or why we feel the way we do we put ourselves in a much better position to get by it and move forward.

I have let fear dictate terms over my actions for far too long. Maybe I didn't attend that job interview not because I was under qualified or too inexperienced but because I didn't have the confidence to talk in front of successful professionals so I lied to myself to escape facing the real truth, I didn't go to the football trial, not because I didn't want too but because I doubted myself too much and thought I wasn't good enough. Chances are I may have been too inexperienced and not got the job; chances are I in fact wasn't good enough on the field, but what if I was?

What other opportunities have we all let slip because we let fear control us?

Where would we be now if we were prepared to look deep within us and find that inner strength and just do it?

Could we be living our biggest dreams?

Well at least we would be living with fewer regrets, knowing we knocked down all in front of us in our pursuit!

As T.S Eliot said "Only those who will risk going too far can possibly find out how far one can go".

Sometimes we act out of fear and don't even know it, it can come upon us in significant moments in work or relationships but sometimes it effects are everyday communications. I recently went to this party on the invite of an old friend. The party was in this huge mansion overlooking the harbor in one of the most expensive and prestigious areas. Straight away I went in with preconceived ideas about what the people would be like, I put labels on them as being rich, smart and successful. Where I would normally be confident and laid back in meeting anyone, all of sudden all these labels had strung fear in my mind, I started thinking I was not good enough to be here, what if they asked me what I do, where I'm from, what I own?

Before I had even met anyone I had put these stories in my head and my confidence was rocked as a result. It only took about 10 minutes to realise they were the same as anyone and no different at all. It's a perfect example as to how we tend to create these stories in our heads based on nothing; but soon they affect everything right down to how we act and our personality.

This fear has the ability to control you; self- confidence and self -belief is absolutely vital in all aspects of life and especially paramount in taking control of our fears so that we can take advantage of any opportunity that presents itself.

Don't look back on life regretting the things you didn't do because you were too scared to have a crack and get outside your comfort zone. Some of the greatest achievements in history come in times of great fear and great uncertainty and the people that were willing to break down these barriers went on to extremely great things in life.

Presence

"It's being here now that's important. There's no past and there's no future. Time is a very misleading thing. All there is ever, is the now. We can gain experience from the past, but we can't relive it; and we can hope for the future, but we don't know if there is one." George Harrison

I have wasted far too much time dwelling on rubbish from the past and thinking of even more rubbish for the future. All these little fantasies and imaginary fiction get created for a tomorrow that just might not come. Yesterday is gone, let it go, take the lessons learnt from it and use them for today.

If you can't be truly alive here and now then you're not living, life is here and anything else doesn't exist, yes, some bad stuff happens but if you can't move on and enjoy your todays then you may as well not be here, because you're just a walking day dream.

These day's people are in such a rush racing through their hectic lives they forget to stop for a second and enjoy. This is evident in the drastic increase in the number of children put straight into childcare at younger and younger ages so their parents can rush back to work to buy their next fast red car.

The whole time neglecting the whole reason they had children in the first place. The children then grow older with the only role models in their life being their teacher at play group and pre-school.

Role models are becoming sparse in children's lives
154

because everyone is running about competing with everyone for rather meaningless material possessions when their so called 'pride and joy' gets brought up and shaped by strangers.

People argue that they do such things in order to give their child or children a better life and a better future, but maybe I'm stupid or missing something here, but wouldn't spending time, teaching, sharing, caring, loving, shaping and a hundred other things be better for your child's well - being and future.

Instead of brandishing them with presents maybe a little presence is required.

How often do we talk to the people we love, really talk? When we are not distracted thinking about something or someone else and we are 100% listening and communicating. I know I am very guilty of this, talking to someone but thinking about what time the cricket starts or something else just as silly.

Do we really have to wait till the weekend when the working week is over to relax and be present, is Monday to Friday off limits to relax, chill out and be present doing the things we love with the people we love.

After a short trip overseas I moved back home to my parents place whilst I sorted out a new job. I was so busy thinking about getting a job and worrying about what I was going to do that I missed out on an awesome opportunity to spend time with my Mum. It's rare that you get the chance to hang out with your loved ones when you're not in rush or not visiting for a special occasion etc. but just hang out in a normal day with no plans and nothing on.

But instead of being present and really enjoying the time we had I was always worrying myself with things out of my control. It would have been just as easy and just as effective if when looking for work I put 100% effort into it right then and there, and then when it was done and out of my control, be 100% present in the next part of the day. Thinking about it doesn't change it; it doesn't make it happen faster, all it does is waste the time you actually do have and that time you never get back.

Even though I was in a lifestyle and environment away from friends and interests, thinking about getting back to it doesn't help at all, it only makes you miss out on the many great opportunities and moments that today's environment can offer.

Clear the mind and be here now, I have wasted far too many opportunities thinking of something else when I could have been making those opportunities then and there. Don't ask the kids how their day was when you're thinking about what groceries need to be bought and what washing needs to be done, yes, your life is super busy and life is going at a frantic pace, but chill out and enjoy it before its gone, or before you're old and realize you don't even really know anything about your friends and family.

"Do what you can, with what you have, where you are" Theodore Roosevelt

Growing Old

"We don't stop playing because we get old; we get old because we stop playing" unknown

We either die young or grow old, but far too many people get old and give up really living. They lose the things that used to drive them and they settle for a life of midday movies and Law and Order re runs. There are only so many times you can mow the lawn in one week and only so many birds you can chase away from your tomatoes.

We need to find hobbies we love when we are young and continue on with them as we grow old, it will stimulate the mind and body and reinvigorate the soul. These hobbies when passed down can then form the frameworks for building great relationships with our children and young friends and family.

Many people have mistaken the term growing up for growing out and there seems to be a direct correlation between this and the hobbies and interests that have continued with them as they have aged. Dusting off the old long board and heading for a wave with your son and grandchild is not only one of those simple things in life that money could never buy but a real chance to actively participate in the life of your loved ones and actually help shape and transform their lives.

Growing old should be spent doing the things you love with the people you love in a place you love. I still find it strange that people are willing to give up their finest years working non -stop so eventually they can retire in a place
157

they love and relax.

In theory it sounds beautiful but in reality it's clouded with many variables. Sacrificing the present for the future is common and it's definitely necessary to an extent, but prolonging your happiness so when you're old and retired you can finally enjoy it all, is a difficult balancing act.

What will be of your health at 65 years old, what about your wife or husbands health, will you still be able to enjoy the things you like, will you be able to go from 60 hours a week work to sitting back with nothing to do, will you even be alive?

There are probably many reasons you can't do it right now, but if you tinker with things and are prepared to make some changes then there's many an option that can bring the future dream to you now.

A big question that is vital for anyone as they grow older is "would the boy/girl you were, be proud of the man/woman you have become?" and if we continually ask ourselves this question over the course of our lives, and can answer it honestly, then the path you are walking will be that much more sweeter.

Have you been able to let go of all your cravings and desires, that of sex, drugs, the opposite sex?

 Do you know what is really important and are you able to tell the truth, most importantly to yourself?

Have you let go of all your inhibitions and are you 100% comfortable with who you are?

If I were to honestly answer these questions, the answer would probably be a no. At times I could say yes, but I can

158

only think how much more satisfaction and overall fulfillment and freedom I would get if the answer was yes, definitively, all the time.

I'm still at times a passenger to my desires, I still lie to myself and I sometimes feel uncomfortable, but growing up gives us chances to shake these and as we each get closer to being able to answer yes then massive weights fall from our shoulders and greater levels of content start to flow in.

Soon, when the answer becomes a confident yes, I think that little boy inside of me might start to be proud.

As we grow old you have to stay true to who you are and make that little kid inside proud of where you are and where you are heading. Do you really want to be that old guy who is constantly winging about their super, about politics and about pensions or that guy who is so caught up in the past and all their regrets that their todays are going missing and their tomorrows nearly extinct.

When you are truly comfortable and content, and have let go of all your worries and of other people's perceptions and concepts, when you know your self-worth and the right wisdom to pass down, you won't have any regrets, only lessons, and you will have a freedom that doesn't come at a certain age or upon retirement you will live with it every day and every night.

And then if you love to watch the midday movie and love a good Law and Order re run, then enjoy it, who cares about other people's opinions, they would probably love to be joining you on the lounge, kicking back with the air conditioner on, with nothing but time, freedom and contentedness.

And if you love to mow the lawn, fifteen times in one week, then enjoy that too, because you have worked hard, you're happy and you deserve it.

Evan Sutter

Life & Death

"I'm the one that's got to die when it's time for me to die, so let me live my life the way I want to." Jimi Hendrix

I was saddened when reading an article in the newspaper about how in a tragic fishing accident three lives were lost when the boat they were riding in capsized in heavy swell. I was then left somewhat confused and troubled when I read on to see that the sole survivor of this terrible accident was then targeted and chastised to the extent that he took his own life some weeks later.

Of course this guy would have been going through extremely difficult times, where people who were once friends and family all of sudden turn into savages seeking blood and answers, hurling insults and threats of revenge and harm, a young man already hurting from the loss of three close mates in need of support is faced with the blame and anger.

He chooses it is all too much and takes his own life, leaving behind a family of his own, a partner and young children. Of course, no one can even for a second start to even think what he must have been going through, the scars still fresh from the accident and the memories and nightmares still ever present, not to mention old friends now wanting their revenge. But was it worth it, because nothing in life is ever permanent, this temporary grief and intense trauma would eventually subside, offering up second chances and new beginnings.

Instead he leaves behind a young family who now face bigger challenges, his one action placing massive pressures
161

on a now single mother with the already daunting task of raising young kids.

Life offers an array of endless options, option upon option; with every little intricate change we make causing ripples along the rest of our lives. People are sometimes blurred by one thing that causes massive grief and large issues and cannot seem to get around it, cannot seem to come to terms with it. They think there are no options or no ways around it and they choose in one single instance to end it all.

But there are always ways around it. We just have to remove ourselves from it for a second, take a deep breath and think for a moment; sometimes this is when clarity presents itself.

It is sad to see a wasted life and in this case this is exactly what it is, some people get their lives taken from them with no choice, suddenly, not a second to say goodbye to the ones they love, not a chance to think about it, not another option available. Beautiful people are taken every single minute of every single day, taken in horrific accidents, in terrible crimes, in catastrophic injustices, yet people just throw theirs away, are we meant to feel sorry for them?

Could this young man and his family not have relocated to a new place for the short- term until the anger had resided, away from the hate, a chance to relax and clear his head, could he not have taken a holiday overseas to reinvigorate the soul and realize there's a whole big world out there not just this small pocket he feels trapped in. Could he have seeked medical help, protection from the police; the options are endless.

Each person deals with things differently, and as an

individual and no one has a right to judge or criticize, but as long as each person realizes there are options and that nothing is ever permanent then opportunities will not be missed.

Worldwide headlines were made when a nurse in England committed suicide after a Radio prank. Everyone had an opinion and was quick to target the radio disk jockeys responsible, they were sent death threats, the radio stations management was targeted, advertisers were quick to end their associations, the DJ's had to go in hiding and police investigations took place.

But regardless of the state of events, the facts, whether it was meant to happen or not, someone chose to end their life. Was it a direct result of the prank, maybe, maybe not, but someone's life ended.

Are we so weak, insecure and shallow that we let other people opinions and judgments of us dictate what we do? Are we void of substance and character? As Mahatma Gandhi said "nobody can hurt me without my permission".

This poor lady might have been ridiculed and tormented for leaking some confidential information to a radio station on the other side of the world, but was it really that bad that she had to end her own life and leave behind a husband and kids. What about a family holiday for six months? The way the world works these days, on her return no one would even recognize her or know her name. Then there's a new job, relocating or just facing it front on publicly, either way none of them are as permanent as ending it all.

Is anything ever that bad anyway? There are always people worse off.

If things are ever feeling that dire and desperate then go get a job for a month. If you are reading this then chances are you have the capacity to gain employment of some type. Then book a flight overseas to a tropical country, picture white sand and crystal clear water, buy a few cocktails and kick back by the pool, meet some new people, clear the mind, surf, fish, eat good food; a week into the trip you will probably forget why you came in the first place.

Politics

"Politics is the art of looking for trouble, finding it everywhere, diagnosing it incorrectly and applying the wrong remedies."
Groucho Marx

Don't worry yourself too much with politics as this will only cause you strain. Politics will always be concerned with making decisions to get votes and any promise of change will only last whilst these votes are needed, but real long lasting change starts and ends with the individuals, if you care enough about something and you are willing to work around the clock with passion and few pats on the back in return, then you are a brave one and are to be commended.

Politics is common everywhere we look; it isn't isolated to the walls of parliament. It's rife in businesses, schools and sporting teams the world over and sometimes it's as much as who you know and not what you know.

In your final year of schooling it is quite a prestigious honour to be named in your First grade Rugby League team. This particular year it included a guy who couldn't catch, tackle or pass; three rather fundamental skills necessary for success. It didn't take Einstein to figure out he got his run because his father owned a few well known restaurants and provided the team sponsorship.

But a lot of the times these things aren't as clear cut and transparent and it may pay dividends to just look a little deeper at a range of things in life and you might get a clearer, more accurate depiction.

165

Scribbles on the Wall: Lessons Along the Way

We can't believe everything we read in the papers and magazines; every story has an angle and every writer some conflict of interest. The big businesses can create anything to appear just the way they want it and it is a great medium to influence and sway ideals. You have to question where the story is coming from and what their motives are, it is becoming rarer and rarer to read an objective piece and this is especially the case when it comes to politics, political parties and elections.

And some of the time stories are written because there is simply nothing else to print. Take this for example; a few years ago my roommate at the time was struggling to find interest from any of the Australian Rugby League teams, with his current club showing little interest also it came to the point where overseas options became the only viable option. With a creative mind and 20 minutes to spare I whipped up an email to the leading sports journalist at the major newspaper in the city to try to drum up some interest.

I wrote of interest from several clubs, local and abroad, even a quick Wikipedia search found some teams from Japan. I wrote contact names and even provided a possible headline.

The very next day, a full page story inside the back page appeared stating he was off to Japan. Later in the morning it was on the radio and by night the T.V.

It just goes to show if they can print a rather innocuous article like this in order to fill up some space there's not knowing what they will conjure in order to get more readers.

This is very much the same with people in general and politicians especially.

166

So just look a little deeper at everything you see, read or hear and don't take things for what they appear to be on face value, because a lot of the time, if not most of the time, things aren't what they appear to be.

It is an ignorant, foolish person who automatically believes what they see on T.V or read in a magazine or newspaper.

So if you want to see real change in your local area, or if you're thinking big and want to make big changes in the world, then don't leave it to the politicians or the CEO, or the celebrities; take action yourself.

If we look backward in time, we see that change does not happen from the government, the industrial, the political level; it comes from the level of individuals. Passionate, courageous, compassionate individuals who love and care about themselves and others, individuals who simply do what they see is necessary and often this can be very simple and fun. They do it with a joy and lightness that is polar opposite to the reactive, burdened movements of a human being forced to live in the heavy shackles obedient to another man's rules.

There's plenty of examples of these hard working, world changing individuals, India had Gandhi, South Africa had Mandela, America had Martin Luther King, Vietnam has Thich Naht Hahn and the oceans have Captain Paul Watson of the Sea Shepherd.

Community

"We are in Community each time we find a place where we belong"
Peter F Block

Playing PlayStation against a guy in China doesn't count as community. We need to get outside and involved in life, the days of playing in the streets with everyone in your neighborhood until the street lights go on needs to be revived for the sake of our next generations. Coming home and playing computer games or jumping on social media is very bad, gone is the communicating with people from all ages and backgrounds and gone is the physical health benefits.

It didn't matter what it was but we were out there getting dirty. Backyard cricket, football, soccer, skateboarding, tennis, tips, running races, swimming, mud footy, roller blading, these are the moments where kids learn the necessary tools to make it in life, these times are more valuable than the six hours they spent prior at school, here they learn confidence, resilience, friendship, communication, independence and self- belief.

It's no wonder there's this big bully epidemic going on these days, people used to get picked on, teased and targeted every day, it's part of growing up and you learn to deal with it, it's like being the youngest child or the guy who always got bowled first ball in cricket, you tough it out and this makes you who you are. People these days are so used to this lack of community and this reclusive nature that technology has created that they are unfamiliar with these environments and people in general. They get picked on once and they can't cope with it and they think it is
168

someone else's fault when really the problem comes from within; and maybe it starts from this fading community present today.

Schools across the planet have played their part in this almost extinct society. Some have rules on no handshaking, no hugging, they make it so kids can't say 'no' if another child asks them to play. They make everything seem so precious and they make young children so precious and vulnerable as a result. As a young child you find common grounds with other kids your age, based on similar interests and skills, these relationships are some of the most important and critical things any person no matter what age can attain.

Instead of developing thick skinned, strong characters full of individualism and substance we are creating weak, insecure, shy kids who can't associate and be representative of any group.

When I was a kid, bullying was around but it was never a big deal, it was simply a part of growing up and I believe it is absolutely necessary in order to build a strong self – esteem and confidence. People are so quick to play the blame game, they get teased and the problem lies with the other person who might have called them a name. But shouldn't we be big enough, confident enough and have enough faith in ourselves to dismiss any slur or insult. As Mahatma Gandhi said, "Nobody can hurt me without my permission".

Some people have a harder time than others and are targeted and bullied far too often but implementing ridiculous measures to outlaw it is fraught with danger.

The biggest single issue when it comes to bullying today is the growth of technology and the plethora of social media platforms. What was once finishing with the sound of the bell is continuing beyond the gates of the school ground and it is a new battle facing all relationships for young people.

But regardless of the method or means of bullying it starts and ends with a strong foundation built at home, breeding confidence and self – assurance in young children is absolutely paramount. We have all been bullied at one stage or another in our lives, it doesn't escape the cool kids or the football stars, how we deal with it makes all the difference.

Playing the blame game doesn't help nor does feeling sorry for ourselves, as with everything in life nothing is permanent.

Parents are massive contributors to this new epidemic, instead of telling their children it's a natural part of life and to stay strong and breeding this much needed self - confidence at home they either don't talk it over with their kids at all or take it straight to the school principal which in turn magnifies the whole thing.

Are we are witnessing a society of insecure, substance less little kids instead of confident, unique individuals?

This whole community is so important for individuals and society in general, we need to provide groups where people can associate with and belong no matter how different they may first appear, groups that harness individuality and unique character, that foster friendship and compassion and create people strong, self – assured and confident.

This could mean joining a local sporting team, a language class, a debating team or drama group, a cooking class, pottery, magic cards, ballroom dancing, archery, a writing
170

class, (I'll need to join that one) a neighborhood watch scheme, an afternoon backyard cricket match, invite the neighbors over for a swim or a BBQ, it all breeds togetherness and association and it's a great way to continually break down the barriers that segregate to many people today.

"The most important single ingredient in the formula of success is knowing how to get along with people" Theodore Roosevelt

Stress

"Life is really simple, but we insist on making it complicated."
Confucius

We love making life more complicated than it should be. We overburden ourselves and overexert ourselves chasing after this imaginary mecca, the big house and the fast car but all too often we get stuck chasing our tomorrows and letting our todays slip away.

Stress kills, everyone can see this but people seem 'happy' to settle for this life of stress, anger and tension. Like our German friend Jeremy from the 'Health and Happiness' section, far too many people are dealing with stress and apply band aid solutions, they think the yoga class will stop there stress, or beers on the weekend, or a holiday but this is only a portion of the answer, creating less stress through living within ones means and living well in the first place is the answer.

Twenty years ago it seemed like ADHD and bipolar didn't exist; now every second person is taking tablets for something or the other. Is it a natural progression? Is technology to blame? Does it even exist, or are we so into diagnosing everything and creating scientific terms?

Are we too busy in the rush of the 'new world' that we don't have the time to make proactive change and delve deeper into why things are happening, instead more than happy to just take a few tablets?

Years ago when a child was energetic and couldn't focus for long periods it was natural, just part of life growing up
172

and we tell them to get outside and release some of their over- abundance of energy, now we tell them they have attention deficit disorder and give them medication. As soon as we feel unhappy we reach straight for the magic pills because we must have depression.

We would all be much better off if we just took the time to find out the reasons for are actions, then not only would we save plenty of much needed funds but also save the harmful effects of continuous medication on our bodies.

My father coined an interesting theory to me regarding people, over-thinking and stress. Of course I can't illustrate this theory by using a direct quote due to the significant amount of expletive language used, but for the accuracy of the recount, please imagine one derogatory word about every four or so words.

People's heads are like bins; you just can't keep putting rubbish into them and expect nothing to happen.

Overthinking about tomorrow or yesterday or what he said or what she meant, what you might be doing next week, how much money you need, or you don't have enough money, or its too hot, it's too cold, I can't believe it's raining. Non- stop chaos of nothingness, for many people stopping the constant running through are heads is impossible, as soon as one thought ends it creates another one and another one and it just flows and flows and flows. Most of the time what we are thinking about isn't even necessary, most of the stuff we conjure in our heads is wrong or doesn't even eventuate. We try to figure out what other people are thinking and in turn make assumptions and judgments which turn out to be well off the mark.

It's a crazy merry go round, 24 hours a day, 7 days a week,

where a lot of people have very little control over their minds.

Can this just keep going on for years and years? Eventually like the bin, we start smelling, we are full of so much rubbish that it is overflowing and we become a mess.

The rubbish bin might seem a little outlandish but it seems today that we are happy to accept stress as a part of life and over- complication and over- thinking as just normal life occurrences. Just how we push our bins to the road each week, we too as individuals need to drop our rubbish off.

Exercise, mediation, new lifestyle approaches, new job, finding a bit more balance, spending more time with friends and doing the things we love are all great ways to reinvigorate and release ourselves from stress, anxiety, depression and the rubbish we constantly hold onto.

Success

"A man is a success if he gets up in the morning and gets to bed at night, and in between he does what he wants to do." Bob Dylan

A man or woman goes to school, we are told to study hard. We study hard and we pass all our exams and we succeed. These marks set us on our path to becoming a success.

A man or women goes to work, we work 5 to 6 days a week, this allows us to borrow money off a financial institution and buy property. We keep on working, along the way attaining possessions that justify our hard work, we borrow more money and we now have investment properties and we are given titles like CEO, Directors, Supervisors and Managers.

We become these titles; we introduce ourselves along with these titles, and we talk of board meetings, outstanding tenders, rosters, super funds and when we have worked many years and gained many possessions and many properties, we have succeeded again.

This is the modern day blueprint for success; sure I left all the moments that take our breath away, our first kiss, our first love, weddings and kids.

Our kids will be given all the appropriate opportunities to continue the cycle and they too will become successful in time. Some will become successful quicker than others, some will be born successful. And when we are old, our prime years gone and our bank balance healthy, we will move from where we worked all our lives to somewhere
175

warm and beautiful and retire. We have succeeded again.

My dad always used to tell us and still does that success is waking up every morning and being able to look at yourself in the mirror and blow yourself a kiss. Maybe the old man's mind is still stained from some over indulgences back in the 'good old days' or maybe what he is trying to say is if every morning you can wake up, look yourself in the eye and be happy with what you are doing with your life, be happy with who you are, happy with the people you choose to surround yourself with, then regardless of your title, job or size of your bank balance you have succeeded.

In today's modern age it is very easy to let this modern day blueprint so to speak take priority. We sometimes are so determined to achieve this label of 'success' that we stay in jobs we don't like or live in places we don't like so we can continue to build our list of objects and appear to be a success to everyone around us.

More focus needs to be put on what Bob Dylan says in getting up in the morning and doing the things we want, of course this may seem impossible and can't be done all the time but we can certainly get closer to it.

Success is a lofty topic and it is difficult to define, because no matter what someone is perceived to have achieved or what he or she seems to have acquired no one ever knows what runs through he or she's head, no one knows how happy they feel or how satisfied that actually are, John Wooden said "Don't mistake activity with achievement." and this is rightfully so.

It is an illusionary label and everyone's definition for success differs and therefore it is unique and difficult to define. But if I was going to attempt to do so I think it would have to be a combination of three quotes by three very different people, Deepak Chopra, Anna Quindlen and Zig Ziglar.

"There are many aspects to success; material wealth is only one component. ...But success also includes good health, energy and enthusiasm for life, fulfilling relationships, creative freedom, emotional and psychological stability, a sense of well-being, and peace of mind."

Deepak Chopra

"If your success is not on your own terms, if it looks good to the world but does not feel good in your heart, it is not success at all."

Anna Quindlen

"Success is the doing, not the getting; in the trying, not the triumph. Success is a personal standard, reaching for the highest that is in us, becoming all that we can be. If we do our best, we are a success."

Zig Ziglar

Thirty Two Down

1. Information & Inspiration. Two vital tools you need in any situation; you need to know your stuff, research, study, train. Know every detail, names, numbers, and dates. But you can't just fill up on the facts. There will be days when you need a little more. Surround yourself with quotes from inspiring people, (Branson, Gandhi, Einstein) pictures of cool places, great stories; Surround yourself with inspiration.

2. Leave your Ego at home. Your ego can be your best friend or your worst enemy, you are going to get rejected at some stage (Colonel Sanders from KFC fame only got rejected 1,008 times before KFC was born) learn to deal with it, no one digs a jerk who can't see past their puffed up chest.

3. Find a good coffee shop. Put your head down and go. Behind every success story is the untold story of 7 day weeks and 14 hour days (and 1008 rejections, numerous business failures, worldwide fame and millions of dollars) if you genuinely know what you want than you won't mind earning it.

4. Don't be afraid to stray from the pack. Find your niche, whatever it may be. When walking a different path you will be sure to face many critics and you can expect doubters (lots of them) but as Einstein once said "Great spirits have often encountered violent opposition from mediocre minds". The new world is here, open minds lead to open doors, and we crave new, fresh and exciting things. Fulfill us and the fortune is yours.

5. Keep Smiling. Sure there are going to be days where you fall into a heap; but at the end of the week if you are not
178

smiling, why are you doing what you're doing?

6. Go to the toilet standing up. Trust me it is an amazing feeling, no straining; no build up, straight out. The Chinese have been doing this for thousands of years and they have silky smooth bowels.

7. Try something completely new, do something nice for someone you don't know, do something you think you can't! If you let old experience guide you, you will only end up where everyone else did. At least this way –even you won't know where you're going!

8. Hug a security guard. We are all guilty at some stage in our lives of cruelty towards these lonely giants, they get spat on; kicked, punched, all they really want is to be hugged!

9. Tell someone you love them, you like them, compliment someone! Your wife, kids, dad, Siblings, that old guy at work, even if you don't , it will make them feel good, and you too! Love is the grease that makes the world go around smoothly.

10. Jump in the ocean. Cool story; Juan Ponce de Leon a famous traveler sailed around the world in search of the fountain of youth, in the end he realised all he had to do was jump off the side of his boat and into the ocean!

11. Turn the TV off. Free yourself from all the addictive ad campaigns and repetitive talent shows. Australia's got talent, the X factor, Australian idol, master chef, masterchef for kids, masterchef celebs and iron chef. Enough already!

12. Sing karaoke sober. It doesn't take much guts to belt out sweet child of mine or a cold chisel classic after ten
179

schooners with a bunch of your mates screaming along. Test your confidence out when you aren't filled with Dutch courage!

13. Say hello to that girl or guy that you never could work up enough courage. Hello that is how simple it is, no cheesy pick up line, no can I buy a drink, Hello!

14. Eat less. As we get older we tend to stop growing up and start growing out. Cut your meals in half, look better and live longer!

15. Grow your hair long and let your beard grow free. For too long society has frowned upon men and woman basking in all their glory! In other words don't let your life be controlled by the perceptions on how we are meant to present ourselves!

16. Learn a musical instrument. The boys will love you when you whip it out around the camp fire on the surf trip and the girls will love you more. More importantly it gives you plenty of time to relax and chill out by yourself

17. Dance like no one's watching and sing like no one hears. Forget what others think, life is too short to worry about embarrassing yourself

18. Be the leader not the sheep. Be the one who drives change and is willing to go out on a limb, it will take you to some pretty interesting places; and you will always be the first to see them

19. Travel, travel and then travel. Make this a compulsory part of your life and always make it a vital part of your yearly calendar. Get your mates on board, your family and when you have kids or nephews and nieces, be sure to take them on some adventures. It's the best education

imaginable.

20. Take your time to find your passion. Don't be rushed into making decisions, take your time especially when it comes to work, find what drives you and makes you inspired, don't just be willing to join the traffic, forge your own path and do something you love

21. Balance. I never knew what this meant when my brother repeatedly told me to 'find the balance', don't live from one extreme to another, it will wear you down and destroy your passion and health

22. Surround yourself with great people. Nothing worse than kicking with people you don't trust and people you can't be yourself with. You will know when you find the real ones

23. Experience, experience and then experience. Get out there and explore all that life has to offer, only then will you know what you really want

24. Skateboard not scooter, Surfboard not bodyboard. Challenge yourself and try something harder, the good things in life weren't always meant to be easy

25. Have a crack. Safety and security aren't always the best options, greater risk come's greater return, if you believe it can be done, than get cracking

26. Get outside. Forget PlayStation and Xbox; get some sun and live a little instead of being a hermit by yourself inside, don't worry what anyone says, it's not good for you.

27. Be real. Don't leave social media as your only form of communication with people, get out and get talking, don't leave it to the plethora of seedy online dating and

networking sites.

28. No regrets. Don't leave any stone unturned; it will only eat you up alive thinking what could have been if only I wasn't so dam lazy

29. Be wary of the outdated. Taking advice from parents and teachers but taking it as gospel is fraught with danger, the world has changed and revolutionized since they were young, what once was is now no longer, the world is different and the game has changed.

30. Donate Blood. It's quick and easy and it saves lives.

31. Everything is inter-related and inter-dependent. What you do now will affect you later and what you do in one aspect of life will cause a ripple effect in another.

32. Stay hungry, stay foolish. In the words of the great Steve Jobs, stay hungry, stay keen and believe in yourself. Stay foolish, people will say it can't be done and facts and figures might back that up, but self-belief and discipline trumps them both.

Concluding Thoughts

"Don't cry because it's over, smile because it happened." Dr. Seuss

It wasn't until I laid all of these topics on paper in front of me that I started to see things a little clearer. In a way I have gained great clarity and a new found perspective and insight. I have realised that I have made a lot of mistakes, I realise that I have been guilty of a lot of wasted time and opportunity and I realise that my writing might not be as good as I think it is.

But it is only when you think deeply and really dissect parts of your life that you get this clarity, when you're open and honest and really see why you acted and why you did the things you did, it's like you're seeing yourself for the first time. I see now that I wasn't a confident, self- assured teenager but insecure and scared, I wasn't a leader but a sheep happy to follow the crowd and fit in as best as I could.

Many of the things that I see now as being the most integral components of life I struggled at and struggled badly at that. I have lacked passion; had no balance whatsoever and I've either been too far in the future or stuck in the past.

So this is what I've learnt;

Just how important balance really is. My brother used to tell me all the time to find some balance and I thought I knew what he meant but in reality it is a lot more difficult.
183

Scribbles on the Wall: Lessons Along the Way

Everything is inter-related and dependent on another. Drugs and Alcohol hits more than just your health and money. It rocks your passion and personality, damages your focus and confidence and destroys your discipline. Which than hits your relationships, work and money, lifestyle, spirituality and faith. Too much of one thing will inevitably sooner or later create a ripple effect down the line and in turn cause chaos in all aspects of life. That healthy balance is vital and what makes it harder is it's different for everybody.

Finding your passion and what makes you tick. I have chased after short term satisfaction and short term fixes all my life driven by laziness and fear. If you just look deeply and follow your heart instead of simply conforming to what everyone else says is right you might be lucky enough to truly do something you love every single day.

Just get out there and involved and experience all of life's amazing intricate beauties. It's through trying and failing and seeing and doing that we find out who we really are and what we like. With every new food we eat or new person we meet, new place we venture to, new book we read or time we bleed, we find out something about ourselves.

Be present. We are all guilty of spending way too much time in our imaginations. We build up our worries from yesterday and our hopes and dreams for tomorrow totally neglecting today. Today is where it's at; cultivating this worry and thought means wasted time and missed opportunities.

AND surround yourself with good people. This is one of those simple things in life that continually brings the most joy. We can't afford to let all of life's distractions keep us from spending time with the ones we love, because after all this is maybe all we have. Playing golf by yourself is fun, so is surfing and fishing, but doing it with good people makes it all that more special. When I think of all the good times I have been lucky enough to have, they always involve the company of family and friends.

We tend to overcomplicate our lives and over worry, we turn little things into big problems that then consume our time and therefore our lives, we need to relax and enjoy what we have now and appreciate it because we aren't going to live forever.

These bodies are not meant to last forever, they get sick, they get old, and the same happens to those around us, I am constantly reminded of how fragile this inner world is and how it can easily be invaded and taken over by bugs that can stake claim and turn this body into a wretched mess. Each day cells are lost in the battle and new ones grow from that which are stronger and more intelligent, but just like a cloud that soon becomes rain, and river and ocean and tea, we too continue on in the world in countless ways.

Exercising, eating healthy and little, reflecting and finding peace, joy and happiness, are time bound for ultimately we see every day that this all changes and it is our relationship to this change that matters most. Can we be solid and stable in spite of all the challenges and difficulties life inevitably bestows upon us? I think we can and we do, if our love is real love, the kind that has no boundaries between what 'I' want and what 'we' want and what 'life' is presenting us right now. But has only 'yes' this is where we are and this is what we must do, because we are 'life'.

I hope at least some of this makes sense, because it is a growing truth in me that every moment is precious, it is how we create a beautiful future and create a wonderful
185

past, it is where everything happens, it is where life is always happening, it's where we must try and be or we miss life.

I cannot help to see how life is a play of opposites. For all you get, you miss out on something, to go means not to come, to buy means to sell, to choose one, means to not choose another. You should enjoy your decision for the adventure that it is.

It is all an adventure.

"Life is an opportunity, benefit from it.

Life is beauty, admire it.

Life is a dream, realize it.

Life is a challenge, meet it.

Life is a duty, complete it.

Life is a game, play it.

Life is a promise, fulfil it.

Life is sorrow, overcome it.

Life is a song, sing it.

Life is a struggle, accept it.

Life is a tragedy, confront it.

Life is an adventure, dare it.

Life is luck, make it.

Life is too precious, do not destroy it.

Life is life, fight for it."

Mother Teresa